Introduction

Interview a cross section of the more than 500,000 volunteer catechists in our country, and you will find an amazing diversity. You can probably find yourself tucked in there somewhere: There are young catechists, middle-age catechists, and old catechists. There are catechists who have been teaching religion for years and rookies who have just signed on. There are those who absolutely love what they are doing and those who candidly admit they do not *know* what they are doing. There are catechists who fear they know next to nothing about the faith and catechists who can recite the *Catechism* in their sleep.

We've met catechists who have been dragged kicking and screaming into the fray, and are now struggling to stay afloat. Not a few are wondering what they got themselves into. We've met catechists who spend hours each week preparing for class, quite unlike the majority who we think prop their teacher's manuals open on the steering wheel on the way to class!

We've met catechists who couldn't say no and those who said no but were overcome with guilt. They now find themselves in a class with twenty-five third graders every Wednesday afternoon!

We've met catechists who run into the parish video library two minutes before class, scrambling to find something the kids might like. We've met catechists who follow their teacher's manual lesson plans to the letter, and we've seen those who—despite all good intentions—will *never* open their teacher manuals. We've met catechists who are burned out and catechists who are on fire. We have met catechists who bring bags of candy each week, and then wonder why the already-wired children are swinging from the light fixtures. We've met catechists whose now grown students still speak with awe about them because of the impact they had on their students. We've met catechists who are catechists today because someone else passed on the faith in an effective and dynamic way when they were children.

In the cross section of catechists we've just described, there are thousands of *reluctant* catechists—people who are giving of their time and their energy, but who are not all too sure about it. They share the reluctant feeling the first disciples had when they went out two-by-two to spread the Good News. Perhaps you are one of these people. If so, this book is for you.

We offer this guide with some thoughts, inspiration, reflection, and practical ideas about who you are as a catechist and what you do as a catechist.

One of the worst feelings a catechist can feel is *disconnected*. So, this is a book of connections. We want you to feel connected—to your ministry, to the lessons you teach, to the students, to the parents, and to the parish. And, of course, we want you to feel connected to Christ and the Church.

You do not need to read this book cover to cover. Pick it up when you need a "pick me up." Consider your venture into catechetical ministry a part of your adventure of discipleship.

A Note on Resources: We are giving you just the title and author for books. That will be enough for you to locate the resources online, in a bookstore, or at the library.

What Do I Do Now?

A Guide for the Reluctant Catechist

Dan Pierson

Susan Stark

Pflaum Publishing Group
Dayton, Ohio

Cover and interior design by
Elaine Tannenbaum Design

Edited by Cullen W Schippe

Fifth Printing: 2010

Pflaum Publishing Group
2621 Dryden Road, Suite 300
Dayton, OH 45439
800-543-4383
pflaum.com

ISBN 978-1-933178-22-6

Table of Contents

Table of Contents ———————————

1

The Catechist Connection

Stop! Take a deep breath! Take another deep breath! Now turn the page and read about yourself as a catechist. Read and reflect on what you have to offer the Church by your presence, by your living faith, even in your doubts and fears and hesitations.

Why Did I Say Yes?

T hroughout the year, there will be times when you find yourself asking, "Why did I say yes?" You may struggle with finding time in an already busy schedule to prepare the weekly lesson. Family, home, chores, children, work, chauffeuring, exercise, sleep, etc. are all part of our daily lives. You wonder how you can find just a couple hours to prepare the weekly lesson.

Then there is the lesson that just did not go the way you planned, and you wonder if anyone learned anything. Presentation of the lesson was challenging, some children were totally uninterested, and only one remembered what was covered in the previous lesson.

And so, sometimes you feel inadequate in not knowing enough about the content of the Catholic faith or about creative ways to develop an engaging sixty-minute lesson.

Rest assured you are not alone. Each week thousands of catechists throughout the country are asking the same questions. Serving as a catechist is a calling. Through your pastor and parish coordinator of religious education, God has called you to announce the Good News. You are helping your children develop an intimate relationship with Jesus Christ and experience the joy of being a Catholic.

Being a catechist is also a growing experience and responsibility. While you, like the Apostles chosen by Jesus Christ, feel unprepared, know that being a catechist is an ongoing journey in faith. It is a time to learn more about the Catholic faith and to develop the confidence and skills to share faith with children, family and friends.

To be called to this ministry, affirmed by the Church for it, and dedicated to it, the work of catechesis is a worthy ministry.
 General Directory for Catechesis in Plain English, 231

As you begin the catechetical year, you may want to subscribe to *Catechist* magazine, published by Peter Li Education Group.

But I'm Not a Teacher!

Perhaps these were your very words when a parish leader first approached you about becoming involved in the religious education efforts in your parish. You do not have to be a certified teacher to be a catechist. Almost a half million people like you volunteer every year in their Catholic parishes to help nurture children and young people in the faith. We would venture to say that most of them are not teachers by profession.

Many people use the two words—teacher and catechist—interchangeably. What is important, though, is how you see yourself. Do you see yourself as a catechist or as a teacher of religion? The two are often used synonymously, but they do have different meanings.

All catechists are teachers of religion. Teaching religion is a part of what you do. You do not have to be a professional teacher to be confident and competent to take on this role. Your parish catechetical leadership provides resources and support that will help you be successful.

However, not all teachers of religion are catechists. Why would this be so? What is the difference? Focus on the goal you have—the primary goal for the students. What is it? Whether or not you see yourself as a catechist depends on this goal.

You might respond that your goal involves helping the children learn more about being Catholic—learn basic prayers and basic beliefs. These are teaching goals, and they are what determine lesson objectives and learning outcomes. However, as a catechist, your main goal is the *growth in faith* of your students. Moreover, that growth involves the *whole* person.

A catechist helps young people explore, in an age-appropriate manner, very important questions. How is God present in their lives? Where do they see the movement of God's Spirit in their homes, their school, their community? How does being Catholic challenge them to live as disciples of Jesus Christ?

_____

A catechist's goal is to help the person being catechized to connect faith with life.

> The catechist is essentially a mediator. He facilitates communication between the people and the mystery of God, between subjects amongst themselves, as well as with the community.
> *General Directory for Catechesis (GDC), 156*

✔ *The Joy of Being a Catechist: From Watering to Blossoming* by Gloria Durka, Ph.D.

Am I Really a Minister?

Yes! Catechists are ministers. It can be both heady and frightening to be told that you are a minister. And you might have moments when you feel like a fraud. "Me, a minister?" It might not have been what you had in mind when you signed up to be a catechist.

Take heart. Catechetics is a process—a pilgrimage, of coming to know, love, and serve God. You are a guide and companion to the young people you are serving in your role as catechist.

Your role as a minister includes the five traditional dimensions of ministry. (Get ready to learn five fancy Greek words, too.) *Kerygma* is the Greek word for proclaiming of the Good News and preaching about Jesus and God's reign. *Didache* is the word for teaching. You help the children interpret the Gospel; you relate the Gospel message to their own life experiences. *Koinonia* is the word for developing community. Simply being a person of faith willing to share yourself with the young people does the trick. Your willingness to tell your story about how God is a part of your life will encourage them to open up and make connections with each other about God in *their* lives. A community of faith naturally emerges from such connections and faith sharing. *Leiturgia* is the word for worship and prayer. Maybe you have never led a group of twenty-two third graders in prayer. Do not worry.

Prayer takes practice, so you and the children can practice prayer together. You and the young people will feel more comfortable and confident praying together as the year progresses. And now for one final fancy Greek word! *Diakonia* is serving others. As a catechist, you are a role model of service to the faith community, and you can encourage a spirit of service among the children you work with.

Perhaps most central in your role as a minister, you are an integrator. This means that you reflect on life, in every aspect, and connect it with faith. There is no separation between faith and life. This happens in your own personal spirituality and in your work with young people.

Being a catechist is accepting the challenge to live faith, to do faith, to practice faith, to grow in faith. You have said yes to the adventure of discipleship.

> The Lord Jesus invites men and women, in a special way, to follow him, teacher and formator of disciples. This personal call of Jesus Christ and its relationship to him are the true moving forces of catechetical activity. "From this loving knowledge of Christ springs the desire to proclaim him, to 'evangelize,' and to lead others to the 'Yes' of faith in Jesus Christ."
>
> *General Directory for Catechesis (GDC), 231*

 I Am Bread Broken: A Spirituality for the Catechist by Howard J. Hubbard

Am I Capable?

"**I** feel like a fake. I'm not qualified to do this." These are common feelings for a new catechist. Many of us, when we first began, had that sinking feeling in the pit of our stomachs: "What on earth am I doing? If they only knew how little I know!"

You may be unsure or insecure about teaching religion, but this does not mean that you are incapable. A theology degree or teaching credential is not a prerequisite for helping form young people in the faith.

Melanie, now a parent with grade school children of her own, still remembers the college student who taught her sixth grade CCD class, not because this particular volunteer had any training (she didn't), but Melanie will never forget how enthusiastic she was about her faith and how much fun she was.

How you interact with the children in your class will have far more impact than what you teach. Sure, you hope they will remember the prayers you teach them That may happen more because of how you pray those prayers together than because of the memory drills! And you hope they'll learn about Jesus' forgiveness. And they will—not just because they read about it in their textbooks but also because they saw and heard forgiveness in you. You will also help them see the need for forgiveness in their own lives.

All this is not to say that what you teach is not important, but being able to recite Church doctrine in your sleep is not necessarily going to help the children see the presence of God in you or in them. Who you are is just as important (and perhaps more so) than what you know. At the same time, you don't have to have it all together as a person either. What are your most important credentials for a volunteer catechist?

- Are you a faith-filled person who cares about young people?
- Are you excited about being Catholic and eager to share your faith with others?
- Do you recognize your baptismal call to share your gifts in service to others?
- Are you willing to give a few hours a week, in preparation time and class time, to invite children to learn about God?
- Are you open to the challenge of learning more about your faith?
- Are you willing to be a model of what it means to be a healthy, caring Christian person living in the world today?

If you can answer yes to most of these questions, then you are capable of being a catechist.

No methodology, no matter how well tested, can dispense with the person of the catechist in every phase of the catechetical process. The charism given to him by the Spirit, a solid spirituality and transparent witness of life, constitutes the soul of every method. Only his own human and Christian qualities guarantee a good use of texts and other work instruments.

GDC, 156

☑ *The Catechist's Companion: Planting, Watering, and Growing* by Cullen Schippe

Flunking Out of Faith

C atechists are not the only ones who might harbor feelings of inadequacy about their knowledge of the faith. Many Catholics do. Talk to any Catholic who has been stumped by a trick question or two. "So why do you people worship Mary?" or "Do Catholics really believe the Pope is never wrong?"

As a catechist, you are a facilitator in a learning environment. And so it is safe to assume that questions will come up—raised either by the children or their parents—that you may not be able to answer. The key here is to realize that you do not have to be able to answer every question. It is perfectly okay to say, "You know, I don't know the answer to that. But I'd love to see what I can find out and get back to you." This response models something incredibly valuable to a child or to another adult. It shows that faith is a lifelong exploration and adventure.

Knowing it all is not the most important thing.

Jesus gave careful attention to the formation of the disciples whom he sent out on mission. He presented himself to them as the only teacher and, at the same time, a patient and faithful friend. He exercised real teaching "by means of his whole life."

GDC 137

 What Makes Us Catholic: Eight Gifts for Life by Thomas H. Groome

I Do Not Know Much about the Bible

L ike the majority of Catholics, you may find that you do not know much about the Bible. There may be many good reasons for that fact. Nonetheless, now is the time to learn a little more about the Bible, to integrate the Bible into your daily prayer, and to make it a part of each catechetical lesson.

Since the Vatican II Council, Catholics have been encouraged to study and read the Bible. In his autobiography, *The Confessions*, St. Augustine tells about his conversion from a life of pleasure, excitement, and love of material possessions. While sitting in the garden he heard a child chanting, "Take and read. Take and read." He opened the Bible randomly to a passage from Saint Paul's letter to the Romans *(13:13-14)*, which urged him to cast aside the past and begin a new relationship with God.

As a catechist you are also invited to "Take and read. Take and read." All good catechetical programs have woven Sacred Scripture into each catechetical lesson at each level. This gives you an opportunity to learn a little more about the Bible as you share the lessons with your class. And don't forget about the Sunday readings. They are a source of study for you, and it never hurts to share them with your students.

In his very popular introduction to the Bible, Steve Mueller offers the following as goals for Bible reading: "Bible reading can deepen our spiritual life. Bible reading can help us change our priorities. Bible reading can help us re-orient our work life. Bible reading can help us find more meaning in life. And most importantly we can meet Jesus again for the first time and come face to face with the God who loves us."

What life can there be without knowledge of the Scriptures, for through these Christ Himself, who is the life of the faithful, becomes known.

St. Jerome, Letter 30

 The Seeker's Guide to Reading the Bible: A Catholic View by Steve Mueller

I'm Not Holy Enough!

Have you had moments of doubt about whether you are spiritually fit to be a catechist—about whether or not you are holy enough? If you have, you are not alone. In fact, some good-hearted people say no to being a catechist for this very reason. They just don't think they are holy enough! What does that mean, anyhow? Is there a checklist or a test to take to determine a holiness score? Of course there isn't.

The fear you experience that you are not holy enough or not spiritual enough is a sign that you take your job as a catechist seriously. And that is a good thing! Here are a few points to consider on how your own spirituality influences your role as a catechist. How do you define *holy*? Many think a holy person is one who goes to church all the time, or whose personal piety seems to demonstrate that he or she has achieved a particular connection to the divine. Could it be, though, that kicking and screaming on the road to faith is a very holy act? Could it be that the doubts, feelings of inadequacy, and struggles with belief are the gutsy kind of stuff from which a true, deep faith is formed?

How do you define spiritual? Are your expectations high for experiencing a lot of warm and fuzzy feelings about matters spiritual? Many of us put up our feeling antennas, and when nothing transmits we doubt we are even capable of making a God connection. A spiritual person has awareness—sometimes subtle and silent and sometimes overwhelming, loud, and persistent—that God is present.

Look for ways to nurture your own
awareness of God's presence in your life.

Your theology is what you are when
the talking stops and the action starts.
Colin Morris

 Paths to Prayer by Robert F. Morneau

I Want to Quit, But I Feel Guilty

Jane had taught third grade religious education at her parish on Tuesday afternoons faithfully for over twenty years. She wanted to quit—not because she did not like the children, not because of any major changes in her life that were going to interfere, but simply because she wanted to quit. However, she could not tell the director of religious education at the parish. "They are always so short on catechists," she said. "They are begging for catechists the week before religion classes start! How can I quit?" Well, Jane did not quit, until nearly five years later when major cancer surgery forced her to quit. Even then, she still felt guilty!

Why is it that Catholics are always feeling guilty—more comfortable with saying yes than saying no? Like Jane, you may try to avoid issues like these. However, a reading of the Gospels shows that Jesus knew when to cut back. He worked with his apostles for approximately three years. During that time, he gave it his all. Yet, he knew there was time for rest. As we read in Scripture, he was always getting in a boat, falling asleep, going to the other side, and taking time away. Jesus knew how to say "not now."

Maybe wanting to quit is a sign that it is time for rest and renewal. Maybe the answer is neither yes nor no—maybe for you the answer is "not now."

> The apostles returned to Jesus, and told him all that they had done and taught. And he said to them, "Come away by yourselves to a lonely place, and rest a while." For many were coming and going, and they had no leisure even to eat. And they went away in the boat to a lonely place by themselves.
>
> *Mark 6:30-32*

 Visit the website www.gratefulness.org.

Calling in Sick

Y ou can count on it! You will feel like calling in sick at some point in your catechetical career. Even if your commitment is one hour, one time a week, there will be times when you just do not want to show up. And unless you have a very good reason, you are not going to feel very good about it.

You will call the coordinator of the religious education program and tell him or her that you cannot make it to this week's class. (Usually these calls are made on the same day as the class.) Everybody knows about the kinds of creative explanations you will use. And now for the consequences: Your entire class of third graders will be given to (or dumped on) the second grade teacher. (Of course, it is too late to find a substitute. Besides, what catechetical programs have a corps of battle-ready substitutes anyway?) Pandemonium will break loose (we were going to say "hell" but thought better of it), and the catechist will survive just long enough to swear to return you the favor—at the first opportunity.

Now take a look at will happen when he or she does just that. The second-grade catechist (note that second grade is a sacrament year—First Communion—so that class is huge) calls in sick. Those students show up in your classroom. You now have an hour with your class, and the second graders. Now, it is not our intention to make you feel guilty (or keep you from taking a day off if you have a good excuse), but we thought we should give you heads up—a big picture—about the decision you might be tempted to make to skip religion class this week.

Okay, we will take the tongues out of our cheeks! The point is simple. If you feel like calling in sick on a regular basis (when you are *not* sick), or generally feel half-hearted about your role, it might be time for a heart-to-heart talk with your DRE. This person will most likely be very good at helping you figure out why you don't want to show up for class, and he or she will be able to lend the support you need to feel confident and competent about your volunteer ministry. There is also the possibility (although it is a lot harder for a DRE to admit this when it means there will be a slot to fill) that this is not the right ministry for you. Perhaps you could better serve the parish or the religious education program in some other capacity.

Your willingness to share in the ministry of the parish is commendable. Finding the right match between your own gifts and the needs of the parish may take some time. Do not despair if being a catechist is not the right fit. Explore the other ministries of the parish.

Now there are varieties of gifts, but the same Spirit; and there are varieties of services, but the same Lord; and there are varieties of activities, but it is the same God who activates all of them in everyone. To each is given the manifestation of the Spirit for the common good.

1 Corinthians 12:4-7

Called and Gifted for the Third Millennium, by the U.S. Conference of Catholic Bishops

The I'm-Too-Old or I'm-Too-Young Excuses

L et's say this right up front! Don't even think about using these excuses not to be a catechist. For goodness sake, how old was Abraham? "When Abram was ninety-nine years old, the Lord appeared to him and said: "I am the God the Almighty." Abraham thought this was rather funny, especially when God told him that he and Sarah would have a child. Remember this scene: "Abraham prostrated himself and laughed as he said to himself, 'Can a child be born to a man who is a hundred years old? Or can Sara give birth at ninety?'" *(Genesis 17:17)*

You have to love the wise (and humorous) perspective of someone like Abraham. Imagine the wisdom and insight that you, in all your chronological giftedness, have to share with children today. Look at it this way: Ours is a wondrous God whom you have had a bit more time to experience!

As for those of you who think you are too young, must we remind you of Jesus' little escapade in the temple, when he was twelve years old? We are not suggesting that parishes recruit twelve-year-olds as catechists, but you get our point. The fact that you are college-age, or in your twenties or early thirties does not disqualify you from sharing your faith with children.

Rethink the excuses. Older and younger adults alike have something to share about faith and life with children.

> Noah was six hundred years old when the floodwaters came upon the earth.
>
> *Genesis 7:6*
>
> Jesus, for his part, progressed steadily in wisdom and age and grace before God and men.
>
> *Luke 2:52*

To wipe away all excuses, read Psalm 1!

Which Bible Should I Buy?

Now that you are a catechist, you may be thinking that you should become a bit more serious about reading the Bible. Yes, you do have a Bible at home—probably more than one! Nonetheless, now is the time to choose a Bible that you can use for prayer and study. So where to begin?

There are many different Bible translations available in various editions and available from different publishers. There are three major categories:
• **Text-only** Bibles with footnotes
• **Devotional** Bibles that in addition to the text and footnotes include prayers, reflections, and meditations on selected passages
• **Study** Bibles that in addition to the text and footnotes may include extensive reading guides for each of the books of the Bible, reference articles, glossary that defines Biblical terms, concordance, and a guide to the Sunday and weekday lectionary.

The main difference between Catholic and Protestant versions of the Bible is in seven books and parts of two others in the Old Testament. For Catholics these books are known as the Deuterocanonical (Greek for "second canon") and for Protestants these books are known as the Apocrypha (Greek for "hidden").

We recommend one of the following translations. For each of the translations we offer a specific edition.
1. New American Bible (NAB): This translation was done by members of the Catholic Biblical Association of America under the sponsorship of the U. S. bishops. This translation is used in the Sunday and weekday lectionary in the United States. It has

excellent footnotes. For a study Bible we recommend *The Catholic Bible: Personal Study Edition,* Oxford University Press (1995). It was revised with a select concordance in 2004.

2. *New Jerusalem Bible* **(NJB):** This Bible has excellent introductions, and extensive notes. This translation was done primarily by British scholars and is highly literary. We recommend the *New Jerusalem Bible.* Doubleday (1985). Select the edition that includes up-to-date introductions and notes rather than the reader's edition.

3. **New Revised Standard Version (NRSV):** This translation is used for study and worship by Catholic churches in Canada and by many mainline Protestant churches. The contemporary and dignified language has attempted to eliminate masculine-oriented language relating to people (not God) wherever possible without affecting the meaning.

4. **Good News Translation (GNT), Formerly Today's English Version (TEV):** This Bible is a very simple, readable, and thought-for-thought translation that puts the Bible into language for every-day people. The American Bible Society publishes a variety of editions.

> It is a great thing, this reading of the Scriptures! For it is not possible ever to exhaust the mind of Scriptures. It is a well that has no bottom.
>
> *St. John Chrysostom*

☑ For online version of the New American Bible: www.usccb.org./nab/bible

What If I'm Not Sure What I Believe?

A catechist was overheard at a catechist training session, "I'm not sure about the Real Presence. I don't know if I really believe in the Eucharist as the Real Presence." More than a few people in the room squirmed. One can hope that the facilitator of the training was able to clarify some basic criteria about being a catechist, namely that holding the core beliefs of the Church to be true is important—why else be a catechist but to teach what the Church teaches to be true?

The question, "What if I'm not sure what I believe?" is a good one; it is a thought-provoking reflection. Tom Peters, organizational management guru says, "If you're not confused, you're not paying attention." And who has not been confused in matters of faith? We think this quote applies quite nicely to the process of religious experience and formation, and therefore to your role as a catechist. A catechist once had this to say about teaching the Trinity to first graders: "I get so confused when I'm thinking about it. I've heard so many different metaphors and analogies, and I get them all mixed up. How am I ever going to explain it to six-year-olds!" We don't have any easy answers to explaining the concept of the Trinity to young children. Your catechist's manual will be your guide in matters such as this. The key for you is to face the confusion so that you strengthen your own faith because of it. To honestly admit a lack of clarity is to take that important step toward fuller understanding. And we bet that more than one saint has gone to the grave still not quite certain about everything in matters of faith.

Faith is worth a struggle, and doubt, unless you let it consume you, is healthy. The healthiest part of doubt is the part that makes you turn to God with a very simple prayer: "Help me believe."

> The beginning of wisdom is found in doubting; by doubting we come to the question, and by seeking we come upon the truth.
>
> *Pierre Abelard*

Why Do Catholics Do That? A Guide to the Teachings and Practices of the Catholic Church by Kevin Orlin Johnson, Ph.D.

Be Not Afraid

*T*his phrase was heard in television and radio news and seen as a headline in the newspapers in the days following the death of Pope John Paul II. They were the words the Pope spoke to the crowds in Poland during his visit there in 1979. Pope John Paul may have been speaking to himself as well as to the people of Poland. After all he was taking on communism—no small feat. On top of that, the weight of responsibility for Christ's Church was on his shoulders. One can imagine him praying over and over again: "Be not afraid! Be not afraid! Be not afraid!"

This is a particularly apt prayer for any catechist, and a new catechist in particular! Catechists bear a responsibility for the one, holy, catholic, and apostolic church. And for an hour a week, the catechist represents Christ and his Church to a classroom full of squirming youngsters. "Be not afraid! Be not afraid! Be not afraid!"

Don't minimize your fears because they are valid, and some of these fears even become reality:
- "I'm afraid they'll be bored to tears." (That might happen.)
- "I'm afraid I am not ready." (No one ever is.)
- "I am afraid I might say or do something wrong." (That is a possibility.)
- "I am afraid I don't have enough time." (No one has enough time, but does the best with available time.)
- "Both the kids and their parents scare me." (Relax and take a deep breath.)

You could make your own litany of fears. The important thing to remember is that your task as a catechist does not depend on you alone. God's grace is there for the asking. The support of the parish is part of the deal. So, be not afraid!

It also helps to have a couple of prayers handy. Few prayers are more adequate than two recommended by the religious writer Anne Lamott: "Help, Help, Help!" and "Thank you, thank you, thank you!"

———————————————

When the weight of your catechetical ministry is bearing heavily on your shoulders, remember the words of Jesus, "Be not afraid."

> Consult not your fears but your hopes and your dreams. Think not about your frustrations, but about your unfulfilled potential. Concern yourself not with what you tried and failed in, but with what it is still possible for you to do.
>
> *Pope John XXIII*

 Reaching Out by Henri Nouwen.

Spiritual Reflection

A s a catechist, you strive to make sure that your students see a connection between faith and life—that they see how religion, faith, spirituality, belief, and life are all intertwined. God made young people with good antennae that are quick to see when people say one thing but do another. These antennae are a blessing because they will demand authenticity of you.

How do you, as a catechist, make sure you are witnessing to the connections—to the relationship of what you believe, what you teach, and the way you live?

Reflective prayer is important. Patricia O'Connell Killen and John de Beer outline a simple process of personal theological reflection.

1. **Choose** a starting point. Focus, on either some aspect of experience, or some aspect of faith, or a passage from Sacred Scripture.
2. **Identify** the heart of the matter.
3. **Converse** by putting experience together with the wisdom of faith (if an experience was your starting point) or by linking faith with a personal experience (if an aspect of faith was your starting point).
4. **Discover** a new meaning and truth to apply in your daily life.

This simple process of reflective prayer can have any starting point. The trick is not to stay at the starting point, but to make sure that you get the conversation going and let that interior conversation go so that you (with the help of God's grace) will begin to make discoveries. Reflective prayer needs to lead to the application of those discoveries to the future—to a clearer understanding and a quicker response to the urgings of the Holy Spirit.

Use your catechetical experiences or the lessons you are teaching as starting points for your reflective prayer.

What path should I choose to live today? How can I discern a direction? How can I ground my decisions in the values that are important to me? Sooner or later life confronts all of us with situations that raise questions like these, questions about the meaning, purpose, and value of our lives. Life experience invites us to reflect.

The Art of Theological Reflection

The Art of Theological Reflection by Patricia O'Connell Killen and John de Beer

Characteristics of an Effective Catechist

There is a boatload of self-help books that give lists of characteristics shared by effective people, happy people, successful people, popular people—and the lists go on. "What might be a list of some of the characteristics of an effective catechist?" we asked. Below is our list. It certainly is not all-inclusive, but review the list. If you wish, choose one characteristic that can serve as a goal for your development throughout the year. Talk with other catechists, meet with your catechetical leader, read, observe, and practice.

Effective catechists—

1. **Know and try to master the subject matter.** While it is not necessary to have completed undergraduate studies in theology and education, it is necessary for catechists to grow in their understanding of the content that is being presented. For example, if you are teaching in a fifth-grade classroom that has devoted the entire year to sacraments, read a book or articles that will enrich your understanding of sacraments.
2. **Know and respect the students.** What are your students' interests? What are their emotional, social, and cognitive abilities? What are the best methods for teaching and learning?
3. **Have positive expectations for success.** Expect children to participate and learn. As a catechist, "get right down to business," while enthusiastically presenting the content in a caring and structured environment.

4. **Prepare. Prepare. Prepare.** Create your own lesson plan for each session. Never wing it! Use the tools you are given and add what you can. It is a simple equation—the better prepared you are the more effective you will be.

5. **Check for understanding, learning, and application.** Our goal is that by the end of each session the children will know, appreciate, and be able to practice the topic that was presented. Throughout the session ask children to tell you what they heard you say, one thing they will tell their parents, and what they will do in the coming week.

6. **Provide an active and well-ordered learning environment.** Children need and welcome structure, routine, and consistent procedures. Write out your expectations clearly and positively, develop rewards and consequences for positive and negative behavior, and communicate expectations and instructions clearly.

7. **Keep it simple.** Don't get overwhelmed by the topics, information, and activities that are offered with each week's lesson. Be selective. Don't try to do everything. Choose only a few strategies to develop the main message of the lesson.

You may well come up with other items for the list. Just remember how your faith community is counting on you to strive to be an effective catechist.

> Without involvement, there is no commitment.
>
> Stephen R. Covey, *First Things First*

Enjoying God and Teaching Creatively: Insights and Ideas for More Effective Religion Classes by Greg Dues

Growing as a Catechist

As you juggle everything it takes to be a catechist and weave all that into your daily responsibilities at home, at work, and in the community, one commitment that could get very short shrift is your commitment to grow as a catechist—to get formation for your ministry.

Jesus' formation of his disciples contains a model for your own formation. Jesus spent time with his disciples in prayer. He taught them—simply and directly. He showed them—through signs and actions. Their formation helped them see what their ministry was all about.

The *National Directory for Catechesis* points out the need for ongoing catechist formation. You probably won't be forced into a formation program, but you have to look for ways to make sure you get formation.

Prayer, spiritual reading, participating in the Eucharist, and informal sharing with other catechists are all good formational activities. In addition, your parishes and diocese probably offer programs that lead to certification for catechists. As you look to what is available, you will need to have a plan. Rely on your DRE or some other catechetical leader to guide you.

The *National Directory for Catechesis* recommends that catechists attend to their own personal and spiritual growth; grow in knowledge of the Catholic faith, tradition and practice;

understand the person of the learner; and develop age-appropriate methods of teaching and sharing faith. Of course, Sacred Scripture should be the very center of your growth and formation.

Just remember to keep your plan simple.

————————————————————

Develop habits for growing as a catechist that work for you. These habits can continue throughout the year.

As we actively engage in our own formation we are preparing ourselves to further the primary goal of catechesis - "to put people in touch, in communion, indeed, in intimacy with Jesus Christ".
General Directory for Catechesis in Plain English, 80

 Catechism of the Catholic Church

Quick Hits

Take "5"
Five minutes, that is. Just to gather yourself, to breathe, to say
a short prayer. Five minutes can work wonders before the
children show up for your religious education class. Come to think of
it, five minutes of quiet and stillness can work wonders just about
anytime you can squeeze them in!

Juggling!
We know life can be a circus. How many balls do you have in the air
at one time? This week, perhaps the religion class you teach tomor-
row afternoon is adding one too many balls, and it's the one you'd
like to drop. No! Wait, stop, and relax! Read, "take 5!" Then choose
to drop a ball that probably doesn't belong in the air anyhow, like
that problem you are worried over which will take care of itself. (Your
religion class probably can't.)

2

The Catechist-Classroom Connection

Okay. That last class was a disaster. "It can't get any worse," you say. "I don't know how to do this catechist thing." Relax. Trust us when we tell you that you are not the only one. There is help coming! In this chapter, we provide a few tips and reminders that will help you feel more at ease in your classroom setting.

Is This a Test?

Some catechists are tempted to teach the wonders of the Catholic Faith as if they were prepping the students for a high-stakes test. They develop a "pass/fail" mentality toward religion. At the same time, we haven't met many parish volunteers who want to be the one to flunk an eight-year-old out of faith formation! Tests are a part of religion lessons. They are often used to determine a child's readiness for a sacrament or to check progress. Determining readiness for the sacraments is the responsibility of parents, the pastor, and his designated leadership. Using religion tests as the measure of readiness addresses a need that the parish leaders have to insure that the students have the basic knowledge of the doctrines that are considered necessary at that level.

Let's take a step back. What is catechesis anyhow? Is it just about head knowledge that can be assessed in multiple choice, true or false, or by matching an item? Or is it about helping a person grow in his or her relationship with God and inspiring that person to the service of others? Actually, catechesis involves all three of the dimensions named above: to **know**, to **love**, and to **serve** God. Catechesis involves the *whole* person.

If you struggle for a balance of the three dimensions, yours is a worthy struggle. Our guess is that you know that knowledge is important, but you also realize that being Catholic is much more than reciting memorized doctrine or prayers.

Through this struggle you will clarify for yourself what it means to nurture children in the faith. And it is likely you will enter into conversations with others in your parish about how faith formation efforts can minister to the whole person.

> Truly, to help a person to encounter God, which is the task of the catechist, means to emphasize above all the relationship that the person has with God so that he can make it his own and allow himself to be guided by God.
>
> *(GDC, 139)*

To Teach As Jesus Did by the United States Conference of Catholic Bishops

Too Many Numbers

W hen the *Catechism of the Catholic Church* was published in 1994, Pat presented it to his seventeen year-old daughter, Mara, for her review. After a quick glance, she responded, "Not interested, Dad. Too many numbers."

The English translation of the *Catechism of the Catholic Church* (second edition) published by the United States Conference of Catholic Bishops has 904 pages, is organized into four parts, and has 2,865 entries.

Since its publication, all major curriculum publishers are required to submit their catechetical programs to the Office of the Catechism of the United States Conference of Catholic Bishops for review and an official declaration that the program is in conformity with the curriculum guidelines and the *Catechism of the Catholic Church*.

Like you, we haven't read all 2,865 entries of the *Catechism of the Catholic Church*. We agree with Mara, "Too many numbers." Rather, we consult the *Catechism* as a source of information, explanation, and reference.

From a catechist's point of view, it seems that publishers are trying to cover way too much material in each lesson of the textbook. Generally speaking, we have only a short period of time to convey the main message of each week's lesson. We must ask ourselves, "What is realistic; what is possible?"

It is for this reason that as you prepare your weekly lesson, it is important to identify the main theme and create a specific learning outcome. Then proceed to craft a lesson using a variety of strategies to convey that message.

In your preparation of the lesson you can consult the Catechism of the Catholic Church *for background education and formation.*

> This catechism aims at presenting an organic synthesis of the essential and fundamental contents of Catholic doctrine, as regards both faith and morals, in light of the Second Vatican Council and the whole of the Church's Tradition. Its principal sources are the Sacred Scriptures, the Fathers of the Church, the liturgy, and the Church's Magisterium.
>
> *Catechism of the Catholic Church, 11*

 The Prologue to *Catechism of the Catholic Church*

Less Is More

L et's be realistic here. Your responsibility as a catechist is to find one meaningful learning outcome for each hour or session that you have with the students. A learning outcome is a statement of what you want the children to know, to do, or to be by the end of the class. For example, "At the end of this lesson my fourth-grade students will be able to name two actions and two attitudes that show Christian service." When you look at your lesson for the day, you may be overwhelmed by all of the concepts or ideas that are presented for you to teach.

Read the planning guide at the beginning of the chapter in the catechist's edition of the textbook. Choose the key idea or objective that you will focus on for the session. Then, read the student text for the lesson. How will its content help you focus on the learning outcome you have chosen? Jot down how you might approach the content with the students. Next, turn back to the catechist's edition. What teaching strategies or tips does it provide for you to help you reach your outcome?

Don't forget to add your own ideas. What is unique about your students that will determine how you choose to approach this subject? What experiences do you have to share? Are there other resources you can draw on? How does other content in the chapter or lesson further illuminate what you have chosen as your key idea or learning outcome for the students?

Choosing one simple, focused learning outcome will focus your preparation and help you bring more confidence and competence to the lesson.

The communication of the faith in catechesis is an event of grace, realized in the encounter of the word of God with the experience of the person.

GDC, 150

 The Introduction to the Catechist's Edition of your religion text

Developing the Learning Outcome

O nce you have selected a learning outcome, you are going to need to develop it a bit. The first stop will be (of course) the catechist's edition of your textbook. It will offer a variety of ideas, suggestions, and resources for developing each lesson.

You want to develop a plan that will achieve the outcome you have chosen. Each textbook series organizes its lessons into various steps or segments. For example:

In *Christ Jesus the Way* (Benziger), the steps are called
  • Invitation
  • Discovery
  • Living
  • Review and Explore
  • Home and Family

In *Blest Are We* (Silver Burdett Ginn Religion), there is a three-step · teaching plan
  • Share
  • Hear and Believe
  • Respond

As a general rule, each lesson plan consists of three sections:
  · Introduction – Exploring Life
  · Development – Sharing Tradition
  · Conclusion – Connecting Faith and Life
Select specific learning strategies and activities for each of the three sections. Choose those activities and resources that you feel are most effective in developing your learning outcome.

It will be helpful if you have your own path through the lesson. Write that path out for yourself, too.

Whatever method is used, all catechesis occurs within the life of a worshiping community. Drawn together by the Holy Spirit, this community gives praise and thanks to God.

National Directory for Catechesis, page 107

☑ The catechist's edition of the series you are using

I Have Only 60 Minutes—
24 Times a Year

T hey want me to teach all of *that!* You may question how effective you can be teaching religion—given your limited time with the children. Relax. Realize that noisy Thomas is not going be another Aquinas by the end of the year, nor is that Teresa with the pigtails going to be named a Doctor of the Church in May. However, because you are a person of faith and because these children will be spending quality time with you (limited though it may be), they will have experienced a relationship with an adult believer. That relationship conveys a good deal of the message.

A woman who taught third grade CCD class for twenty-five years had this to say: "For me it was never about how much information they'd walk away with at the end of the year. Sure, I wanted them to know the basics. But I also wanted them to have fun, and to spend one hour a week with a group of peers and myself who shared one important thing in common: We are faithful Catholics." The number of former students who showed up at this woman's funeral was amazing. They were not there to celebrate remembered Catholic doctrine.

Those former students appreciated the 60 minutes,
24 times a year this catechist had spent with them,
and they showed their love and gratitude in return.

> No methodology, no matter how well tested,
> can dispense with the person of the catechist
> in every phase of the catechetical process.
> The charism given by the Spirit, a solid spiri-
> tuality and transparent witness of life, consti-
> tutes the soul of every method.
>
> *General Directory for Catechesis, 156*

 National Directory for Catechesis, page 235

ABC's–Preparing for Sunday

The Lectionary is a book that contains the Scripture readings, including the Gospels, which are read at Mass. The present Lectionary was introduced in all churches throughout the world on the First Sunday of Advent, 1971. The Lectionary contains a structured and planned system of readings that "provides the faithful with a knowledge of the whole of God's Words, in a pattern suited to the purpose" (*Constitution on the Sacred Liturgy, 60*).

The Sunday Lectionary is organized over a three-year cycle with different readings for each Sundays in Years A, B, and C. Then the cycle begins all over again. For each Sunday there are three readings— one from the Old Testament, one from the Epistles or Book of Revelation in the New Testament, and one from the Gospel. The liturgical cycle begins with the First Sunday of Advent. With the exception of Advent, Lent and Easter, there is no single theme that unites the three Sunday readings.

An increasing number of people use the Lectionary as a basic resource and guide for daily prayer and devotions, for Bible study and RCIA programs, and in published catechetical programs.

As you review your curriculum materials you may see a strong integration of the Lectionary throughout each lesson. We know your time is limited, but it would be ideal to take a few moments each week to introduce the readings for the coming Sunday—even if only the Gospel reading. Suggest reviewing the readings as an excellent faith-sharing activity at home.

Through sharing the Sunday readings you and your class can better understand the Word of God and grow in relationship to Christ, his saving activity, and his Church.

> In the Lectionary "the treasures of the Bible are ... opened up more lavishly so that a richer share in God's Word may be provided for the faithful."
>
> *Constitution on the Sacred Liturgy, 51*

 The Web site: www.preparingforsunday.com

Say What?

You know the feeling. You have just stood on your head to facilitate a dynamic discussion with your class, and you are rewarded with blank stares—and silence. Not that silence is a bad thing, but not *now!* Now things get blurry. You try to shift gears, try a different tack, and try some more questions. Before you know it you are drowning in a sea of disinterest!

There is an art to asking effective questions, questions that will stimulate a class. Check up on yourself:

• Is what I'm asking related to the lesson objective?
• Am I expressing myself clearly? Does the class understand the question?
• Is my question suited to their level? Or is it way over their heads? (*Hint:* If you ask questions that would stump a doctor of the Church, don't expect much of a response.)
• Are my questions open ended? For example: "What would you have done if you saw what the Good Samaritan saw?"
• If my question is meant to gauge how well the class can recall what they just learned, am I sure they're equipped to answer it? Do I need to review with them? (There is the catechetical urban legend about the catechist who flipped to the wrong page and was reviewing the wrong chapter!)

Invest some time and energy to work on the skill of asking effective questions. Reflecting on your questioning strategies will also help you develop good questioning skills.

Some Children's Answers to Sunday School Questions
Noah's wife was called Joan of Arc.
The fourth commandment is "humor your father and mother."
Lot's wife was a pillar of salt by day and a ball of fire by night.
The patron saint of travelers is Saint Francis of the sea sick.
The first commandment was when Eve told Adam to eat the apple.
It is sometimes difficult to hear what is being said in church because the agnostics are so terrible.

Source Unknown

✔ *How to Talk so Kids Will Listen and Listen So Kids Will Talk* by Adele Faber and Elaine Mazlish

Creating Creativity

At a catechist training session, we heard one catechist's lament. "I am so not creative. I think the kids in my class must be bored to tears. I know I am." She laughed, but it was one of those "this isn't really very funny" laughs.

We have found that it is much easier for a volunteer catechist to be creative in the classroom when he or she has planned for creativity in advance. This might sound odd, but spontaneity and creativity don't necessarily go hand-in-hand. Volunteer catechists need to create their creativity.

Create an art supply box. Fill this box with art supplies—glue, markers, crayons, glitter glue, glitter, watercolors with brushes, poster paper, scissors, yarn, tissue paper, clay, envelopes, a paper punch, index cards, clear contact paper, old magazines—anything and everything you can think of that might come in handy for a spur of the moment craft project.

Create a costume box. Use your imagination (or the imagination you had when you were the age of your students) for this box. Fill it with clothes and other items that children can turn into costumes for role-playing and skits.

Scavenge. Great places to scavenge include other people's class-rooms—other catechists and teachers are great resources for ideas that work (and they can alert you to ones that don't). Use the Internet. There are sites with teaching activities. Granted, they are not all related to religious education, but sometimes all it takes is a kernel of an idea to get the juices flowing and to make an easy adaptation to your curriculum.

———————————

Don't forget magazines. Many have seasonally-based activities that you can adapt for classroom use. Keep a file folder for the ideas you clip out of magazines and other resources.

> The principal goal of education is to create adults who are capable of doing new things, not simply of repeating what other generations have done—adults who are creative.
>
> *Jean Piaget*

Jump Starters: Quick Classroom Activities that Develop Self-Esteem, Creativity and Cooperation by Linda Nason McElherne

Keeping Your Cool

"Sometimes they're just out of control." The catechist was talking about her fourth-grade class. "But then I realize that I'm the one out of control. I just don't know how far I can go in disciplining them. What am I expected to put up with? By the time I get the group to focus, and I practically have to do magic tricks standing on my head to get their attention, time is up."

This particular catechist knew that her students, who met for religious education on Wednesday afternoons, had already been in school all day. So she wanted to cut them some slack, but in doing so had lost all control. What's a catechist to do?

A good rule of thumb is that if you don't tolerate certain behaviors in your own home, don't accept them in the classroom. In other words, if you wouldn't let a child swing from the light fixtures (okay, we're exaggerating) or sit on the tables in your home, don't allow them to in the classroom. If you don't allow your own children to pop softball size bubble-gum in your face while you're talking with them at home, the behavior isn't acceptable in the classroom either.

The key is to establish the rules upfront and to communicate the expectations you have. Begin the year with ground rules. Let the group help you articulate what these rules should be. Use cooperation, respect, and shared responsibility as ways to enforce the rules. Always follow through with what you say you will do. Be fair. Every outburst doesn't necessarily have to become a crisis situation; yet these situations can become a crisis if you overreact, and students will get used to you blowing things out of proportion.

Then, their reaction is to "blow you off." (Translation: They'll ignore you.)

Be there at the door at the beginning of class to welcome the children by name to establish a connection and rapport with them.

_____

Relax. You will find your stride.

> A diversity of methods in catechesis does not detract from its primary objective—evangelization and conversion to Jesus Christ—nor does it dilute the unity of faith. Perfect fidelity to Catholic doctrine is compatible with a rich diversity of presentation.
>
> *National Directory for Catechesis, page 96*

✔️ *The Discipline Guide for Children's Ministry* by Jody Capehart, Gordon West, Becki West

Multiple Intelligences for Dummies

The theory of multiple intelligences is all the rage in education these days. You may have seen references to it in the catechist's edition for your textbook series. Do you have to be an expert on multiple intelligences to incorporate them into your lessons? "I have to incorporate all those different ways that the children learn in addition to everything else I have to do? Yeah, right." Before you panic, remember that each curriculum is most likely to reach all learners. Nonetheless, a basic understanding on your part is helpful.

Dr. Howard Gardner, a professor of education at Harvard University, developed the theory of multiple intelligences in 1983. It suggests that the traditional notion of intelligence, based on I.Q. testing, is far too limited. Instead, Dr. Gardner proposes eight different intelligences to account for a broader range of human potential in children and adults. These intelligences are:

- **Linguistic intelligence** ("word smart"): Connect whatever you are teaching with words and sentences.
- **Logical-mathematical intelligence** ("number/reasoning smart"): Connect your lesson with numbers or logic.
- **Spatial intelligence** ("picture smart"): Connect your lesson with pictures or videos.
- **Bodily-kinesthetic intelligence** ("body smart"): Connect your teaching with physical activity.
- **Musical intelligence** ("music smart"): Sing about the lesson or listen to music.

- **Interpersonal intelligence** ("people smart"): Make the lesson a more social experience.
- **Intrapersonal intelligence** ("self smart"): Allow time for reflection.
- **Naturalist intelligence** ("nature smart"): Provide some experience of the natural world.

Your catechist's manual will be a great help in suggesting activities suited to the multiple intelligences.

> You don't have to teach or learn something in all eight ways, just see what the possibilities are, and then decide which particular pathways interest you the most, or seem to be the most effective teaching or learning tool.
>
> *Thomas Armstrong*

✔️ *7 Kinds of Smart: Identifying and Developing Your Multiple Intelligences* by Thomas Armstrong, Ph.D.

Creating a Learning Environment

Almost all catechists will meet with children in some type of classroom setting. This may evoke in the students both the positives and the negatives of their Monday-through-Friday schooling. Those parishes without a school may have a learning center with multiple purpose rooms. No matter what classroom space you have, your challenge is to create an environment that is conducive to prayer and activity as well as a positive learning experience.

Here is a list of hints for creating a positive learning environment:

- Maintain a climate and tone of warmth, community, and safety. The space should help children feel welcome both as individuals and as a community.
- Make the room as comfortable as possible and provide space for whole group activity, small group projects, and individual work.
- Be sure that everyone (including you) knows everyone by name as soon as possible.
- Foster a sense of schedule and routine in the space.
- Establish expectations about the ways the class will learn together.
- Create displays that celebrate the children's work and connect to meaningful understanding and application of the lesson of the week. Be sure to coordinate any displays and decorations with other catechists using the space.
- Make your personal demeanor and behavior part of the atmosphere. How you treat the students, how you talk to them, and how you handle yourself will help foster a good and creative environment.

In the catechist's editions for most textbooks there will be a section on learning environments and dynamic teaching and learning strategies. You may also want to meet with other catechists and the director of religious education to develop common procedures.

> Children need uncluttered spaces to do their work and clear, safe pathways for moving about.
>
> *Marlynn Clayton*

☑ *Classroom Spaces that Work* by Marlynn K. Clayton and Mary Beth Forton

Google

The most popular search engine on the Internet is Google. When we are looking for information, seeking an answer to a question, or are just curious about a topic, we simply "Google!"

Over time, that makes us feel connected and encouraged knowing that we have an online resource that will lead us to the answers we need.

As a catechist, you are committed to sharing faith with a group of children, youth, or adults. And to do this successfully and effectively we realize that you too need to grow in your understanding of the faith, in the knowledge of those you teach, and in creative and effective methods of teaching.

Your catechist's edition will provide excellent background material for each lesson. You can gather with other catechists to share ideas, ask questions or discuss an article or chapter from a book. You may also want to seek the support and information from your catechetical leader or pastor.

In addition, we encourage you to Google your questions or requests for information. With Google (or any other search engines you might enjoy), you have a personal Help Desk for your catechetical ministry.

The search engine is a tool that will lead you to information and resources on the content and practice of the Catholic faith, teaching methods, history of the Catholic Church, commentary on the Sunday and daily Lectionaries, and so forth. In addition, there are many Catholic information Web sites that you can bookmark and keep handy for quick reference.

There are many technological helps that will keep you connected to your lessons.

> When one teaches, two learn.
> *Robert Half*
> Who dares to teach much never ceases to learn.
> *John Cotton Dana*

A searchable, online version of the *Catechism of the Catholic Church* at: www.scborromeo.org/ccc.htm

The First Session

*I*t may be a few weeks ago or even last spring that you volunteered to serve as a catechist. Now the day for your first session has arrived and you realize that you are nervous and possibly for a brief moment you wonder if you should call in sick. Recognizing that there is no turning back, you pray the reluctant catechist's prayer, "Help me! Help me! Help me!"

Here is a little script to help you with that first session.
- Review your printed lesson plan. Gather together the supplies and resources that are needed.
- Prepare a personal outline of the class session, indicating the outcome and the main learning activities.
- Arrive early—at least 60 minutes before the start of the first class and then a minimum of 30 minutes for subsequent classes.
- Arrange the seating in the room.
- Position supplies, paper, books, and resources in the order of use during the session.
- Check in with the catechetical leader for announcements, directions, procedures.
- Take a deep breath, get focused, and turn the class over to the "Master Catechist."
- As children begin to arrive, introduce yourself. Welcome them to the room and have them prepare a name tag and select a seat.
- Once all have arrived and are assembled, formally introduce yourself, share personal information about yourself, family, children, and interests. Encourage good attendance.

Proceed throughout the lesson as planned. At some point you may want to take a break. Depending on age level, facilities, and resources, you may want to take a short five-minute break within the room.

After class and before you leave the room, jot down on the back of your lesson plan any notes, ideas, concerns, etc. that you may find helpful in the future. And then pray once again by saying, "Thank you! Thank you! Thank you!"

> Those who with God's help have welcomed Christ's call and freely responded to it are urged on by Love of Christ to proclaim the Good News everwhere in the world.
> *Catechism of the Catholic Church, 3*

✔ Become thoroughly familiar with the catechist's edition. You will find a wealth of ideas, suggestions, and resources for planning your first session and all the rest.

Quick Hits

Copy, Cut and Paste
This is an amazingly useful strategy. You may already be doing some of this. Did you know that many long-time catechists copy, cut, and paste on a regular basis to put programs or lessons together? It is a way to be creative when you are stuck and don't know quite how to approach a particular topic, or when you want to put a little of *this* lesson together with a little of *that* lesson to better fit the learning needs of your students.

The Catechist's Edition
Open it. Read it. We are not suggesting you read it cover to cover in one sitting. However, do scan the table of contents and find some time to review what is in there. Many of the good catechist's selections are toolboxes full of useful information–insights that will help you be more effective. They also offer many practical strategies.

Bringing the Lesson to Life
One way to do this is to "let **you** shine through." If the children see and feel your enthusiasm, the lesson will be sure to have life. Don't be afraid to bring your passions into the classroom. One woman, who was somewhat musical and played the guitar, started every class by playing a fun melody on her guitar while the children made up (ad lib) a song about the theme or topic for the day. Not only did they all have fun, but it served as a great focusing activity, and it gave the catechist insight into what the children knew about the lesson's topic by the lyrics they chose. Incorporate your gifts into your teaching!

3

The Catechist-Child Connection

"Who *are* these kids, anyway?" Or here's another one: "What's the matter with kids these days? They're so different than we were." Yes, and no. Certainly a big (okay *huge*) part of being a catechist is connecting with the children you teach.

We do not intend to give you a crash course in child psychology, but we do have suggestions for practical ways to more effectively reach the children in your class.

Who Are These Children, Anyway ?

"My parish needed a fourth-grade catechist, so I volunteered. But I don't know a thing about fourth graders!" Sound familiar? Maybe you have (reluctantly) volunteered to take on a class of children and find yourself wondering just who they are. What do you know about nine-and ten-year-olds? Awareness of the developmental characteristics of the children you are teaching will help you meet their learning needs.

A teacher of a sixth-grade religion class approached a presenter at a religious education conference. She was teaching this grade level for the first time and felt like a failure. Her class met for one hour after school on Wednesdays. "The kids are just out of control," she said. "I cannot get them to sit still for the life of me! We are supposed to be reading all this information about the Old Testament, but the kids can't focus. They're climbing the walls."

The speaker did not want to tell this faithful volunteer that she just might be setting herself up to fail. He took another approach. He reassured her and told her that what she was experiencing was typical behavior for that age group. Middle-school age children need to move. To ask them to sit still for an hour after they have already spent the day in school is not reasonable. "They are hard-wired for wiggling," he told her. "A basic developmental need they have is the need to move. They are full of energy, and full of creativity. The key is to involve them in their learning."

Very quickly, the two brainstormed a few ways that she could actively involve the young people during the hour. He reminded her to review the lesson ahead of time and look for optional activities in the catechist's edition which would help bring the lesson alive for her particular group. The speaker also added that children at this age long to belong and they are looking for adult role models. He suggested that she slowly get to know each of them and that she always greet them by name, both inside and outside of class. She walked away feeling more hopeful, empowered by her new knowledge that what she had been experiencing was normal, typical behavior.

Most religious education teacher manuals contain child development information about the particular age at that grade level. Read this material. At the least, you will know what sort of behavior you might expect. At the most, you will apply the knowledge to your approach with the students.

> We worry about what a child will become tomorrow, yet we forget that he or she is someone today.
> *Chip Wood*

Yardsticks: Children in the Classroom Ages 4-14, A Resource for Parents and Teachers by Chip Wood

Making the Most of Media

Many catechists have had to admit that when faced with a difficult lesson, they have reached for the latest video (depending on the state of the parish library, maybe a "not-so-latest" video). There is always the hope that by the time the video is over, some connection to the lesson will become evident! And so the video is often the substitute teacher for the day.

Media pieces are valuable tools in the religious education setting. With a bit of thought and planning, they have the potential of bringing topics to life, of dramatizing important points, and of reinforcing the central lesson you are teaching. Videos, recordings, readings from magazines, or clips from movies or television shows need to be used intelligently.

Often, media are good ways to open the class. Other times, the media can jumpstart a discussion. Music and video can also be part of a classroom prayer experience or celebration. It is your job to set the scene for the video—helping the students know what to look for. And always provide some opportunity for your students to talk about what they have watched or heard.

You can't do that unless you preview the piece to make sure that it is appropriate. When using popular media, be aware that most movies and television shows are not produced with catechesis in mind. You will need to take care to make sure that your students know why they are watching. And they should always be given the chance to unpack what they have experienced.

No matter what media selection you use, clarify the message and put it in the context of the lesson about the Faith that you are presenting.

Along with traditional means such as witness of life, catechetics, personal contact, popular piety, the liturgy, and similar celebrations, the use of media is now essential in evangelization and catechesis.

The Pastoral Instruction on Social Communications, Aetatis Novae, 11

The Center for Media Literacy, www.medialit.org or the National Institute on Media and the Family, www.mediafamily.org

What's a Catechist to Do?

orty years ago I went into my first classroom as a catechist. That year I taught eighteen third graders using the catechetical series entitled *On Our Way* by Sister Maria de la Cruz Aymes, HHH. For sheer survival, I followed both the student text and catechist's edition slavishly. It was a great year.

The following year, I taught a multi-aged group of twelve boys in grades two through five. What a difference! I was challenged to maintain interest and keep the attention of the group made up of youngsters with vastly different intellectual, social, and emotional needs. I was often discouraged and overwhelmed, and I made it through the year only with the support of other catechists and God's grace.

Last year I taught a group of sixteen eighth graders who were preparing for the celebration of the Sacrament of Confirmation. Now I come with training, a state teaching certificate, years as a secondary teacher, and a graduate degree in religious education. I knew that I was well prepared. But to my surprise and shock I found the year's worth of Sunday-night classes an ordeal. Parts were enjoyable. I love working with young adolescents (I think). As individuals they are enjoyable and energetic. As a group they can be challenging, disinterested, and even a bit defiant.

What's a catechist to do? As a catechist you are given a framework—
· Assignment to a specific class
· A specific class time
· Probably a text and a teacher's manual—often with more content than you can possibly fit into an hour

· Students who (along with their parents) are often over-scheduled, tired, frazzled, bored, or all of the above.

So what does a catechist do? His or her best! A catechist has to be a realist. You will be meeting the needs of the children if you can provide the following—even in the face of less than ideal conditions:

· A predictable sequence of meaningful activities that are age-appropriate and challenging and that include time for quiet and reflection—in short, a well-planned lesson
· A routine greeting time (for conversation and shared interest) and some group activity that builds community through active participation
· A community atmosphere in which we all know and use one another's names, get to know each other's interests and feelings, take turns, share, cooperate, and solve conflicts
· A closing activity or ritual that puts a sense of accomplishment as a punctuation mark at the end of class

---

No lesson will be perfect. Just faithfully do all you can to create an environment in which children can grow in faith, in friendship, and in relationship with Christ Jesus, the Way, the Truth, and the Life.

And God has appointed in the church first apostles, second prophets, third teachers.

1 Corinthians 12:28

 National Directory for Catechesis, USCCB, pages 202-205

Keep 'em Laughing

S tudies indicate a direct correlation between laughter and health. Without getting into specifics, the general idea is that laughing is good for people. This shouldn't be a news bulletin, but a fly on the wall during many parish programs might come to the conclusion that laughter has been banned! So, what is the point?

Have fun. Lighten up. Matters of faith are serious, solemn, and maybe even heavy at times, but they are also full of joy. Joy is the hallmark of the holiest of holy people. Religion class does not have to be an agony in the garden or two days in the tomb. We've got to be able to experience a bit of resurrection and "alleluia" happiness with the children. Would you accept an invitation to discipleship if it were nothing but dull, dark, and (well) lifeless? No. Of course you wouldn't, and neither will the children you teach. Children are fun and full of spirit, as one catechist wryly put it, "full of vim and vinegar."

Have fun!

> Mirth is God's medicine. Everybody ought to bathe in it.
>
> *Henry Ward Beecher*

☑ *The Laughing Classroom: Everyone's Guide to Teaching with Humor and Play* by Diana Loomans and Karen J. Kolberg or *Laughing Lessons: Ways to Make Teaching and Learning Fun* by Ronald Burgess

Praying with Children

In any group of children, a catechist will find a wide divergence of experiences with prayer. Some children will have experienced regular prayer in their homes; others will not. Some children will participate frequently at Mass and prayer services in the parish; some others will not.

If from the beginning of your time with them the children experience you as someone who guides them in prayer, they will quickly become comfortable with the patterns of prayer you establish. While a prayer to open class and another to end the class is appropriate, these should not be the only times you and the children pray together. Prayer is just as important a part of a child's formation as mastering ideas, dates, or doctrines.

Make time for prayer a natural part of every lesson. Try to avoid saying, "Oops! I ran out of time for prayer!"

Look for ways to help the children be comfortable with silence as a way to pray. Certainly you won't be successful with this at the end of a raucous role-playing activity, but there ought to be other quiet, reflective times in your learning session where moments of silent prayer will be appropriate and natural.

Children are much more comfortable with spontaneous prayer than adults are. Encourage this kind of prayer. Let them share their hopes, dreams, fears, and needs with one another and with God. Help the children listen to God by using simple, guided meditations.

(Don't expect them to be able to sit still with their eyes closed for too long!) Incorporate music and movement into prayer, and use images and symbols. In fact, let the children create the prayer space! Setting aside a special part of your meeting space helps nurture a sense of sacred space.

Setting aside time to pray with your students helps nourish their sense of the sacred.

> Prayer is nothing else than a sense of God's presence.
>
> *Brother Lawrence*

☑ *A Book of Ritual Prayers: 30 Celebrations for Parishes, Schools, and Faith* by Jerry Welte and Marlene Kemper Welte or *Children and Prayer: A Shared Pilgrimage* by Betty Shannon Cloyd

Here Comes Everybody

Most catechists are assigned a group of twelve to fifteen students usually of the same age or grade level. The first afternoon the kids come tumbling into the classroom, you just may identify with the statement of the Irish author James Joyce. His famous definition of the Church was, "here comes everybody."

As you get to know a little bit more about each child in your care, you will realize that even within this small group of children there is a great variety of experience, knowledge, and practice of the Catholic faith. In addition some children come with special needs including attention deficit disorders, hyperactivity, dyslexia or other struggles with reading and communication, behavioral challenges, or other learning disabilities.

Learning disabilities are neurobiological disorders that interfere with a person's ability to store, process, or retrieve information. Children with learning disabilities have average or above-average intelligence, and many are gifted, but learning is challenging for them.

The federal law defines a learning disability as a "disorder in one or more of the basic psychological processes involved in understanding or in using spoken or written language, which may manifest itself in an imperfect ability to listen, think, speak, read, write, spell, or do mathematical calculations."

You may not be immediately aware of children with difficulties or learning disorders. A parent may (or may not) share with you—the catechist—what is a major difficulty within the family.

You will have your suspicions, but in a catechetical situation be very careful with the way you address students who seem not to be "with the program." Never level the charge of laziness or inattentiveness. When you vary your activities and your presentation, when you are patient and caring, when you are focused on the children's needs not your own, then you will do well even with children who have difficulty learning.

Remember that Jesus the teacher has called you to welcome all God's children into our community of understanding, care, and love.

> The habits of a vigorous mind are formed in contending with difficulties. Great necessities call out great virtues.
>
> _Abigail Adams_

 A Mind at a Time by Mel Levine, M.D.

More on the Learning Disabled

There are many different estimates of the number of children with learning disabilities. It is reasonable to estimate that 5% to 10% of persons are affected.

The following suggestions provide an introduction to effective strategies for working with such children. These are meant to make you more aware, not to provide a complete set of guidelines. Check your catechist's guide and ask your catechetical leader for additional information and resources.

1. Remember the existence of multiple intelligences. Present all lessons using a variety of strategies—visual, auditory, movement, tactile, etc.

2. Look for help—information and resources that will help you spot the signs and work with the children.

3. In class, keep reading and writing assignments short and then reinforce them with other types of activity.

4. Alternate quiet and active time in the class. Have short periods of each. Make gestures and movements as purposeful as possible.

5. Give oral as well as written directions for all assignments. Check for understanding and comprehension.

6. Some children prefer to do their work in a quiet and uncrowded corner of the room. Allow for that.

7. Create small work groups of three to four children, including in each group no more than one child with a learning disability.

8. Give children specific questions to guide their individual reading. Use markers for highlighting main points.

9. Motivation is found in activities and tasks that initiate, direct, and sustain goal-oriented behavior. Always build in student interest. Reinforce positive results.

———————————————

Your goal as a catechist is to provide the best environment possible for children with special needs. You are showing them the welcoming love of the Gospel.

Let the little children come to me, and do not stop them; for it is to such as these that the kingdom of God belongs.

Luke 18:16

LD Online (www.ldonline.org): An interactive guide to learning disabilities for parents, teachers, and children

Raising Catholic Children

Many catechists are also parents. We cannot help but reflect on how to raise Catholic children. We want for our children what any Catholic parent wants out of a catechetical program.

All of us are overwhelmed by the "busy-ness" of our lives as we meet our responsibilities of work, family, parenting, errands, etc. There seems to be so little time and energy for sharing faith with children and getting them to the weekly parish religious education program.

Julie Cragon, author of *Bless My Child: A Catholic Mother's Prayer Book*, prays that her children will be nourished and fed and led by the light of Christ, his mother, the saints, and the holy men and women given to us as examples. Julie and her husband are parents of six. They are also the managers of St. Mary's Bookstore in Nashville, Tennessee. They believe that praying for our children is one of the most important things we can do for our children.

As a catechist, you can bring your young charges to prayer, too. Remember each one by name and pray that they recognize God's invitation to be His children and friends.

Therese Borchard, author of *I Love Being a Mom,* looks to her parish and the catechists for help in passing on a sense of tradition and continuity with the past. She sees catechists as the bridge of the past with the present—translating the language of faith for children.

To accomplish this mission, we
- Promote knowledge of the faith
- Provide liturgical education
- Offer moral formation
- Teach children to pray
- Read, teach, and pray Scripture

In your weekly lessons, join the members of the Church—parents, extended family members, Baptism and Confirmation sponsors, grandparents, and the entire parish community in helping these children to grow in friendship and intimacy with Jesus Christ.

> The definitive aim of catechesis is to put people not only in touch, but also in communion and intimacy, with Jesus Christ.
>
> *Pope John Paul II, On Catechesis in Our Time*

How to Raise Good Catholic Children by Mary Reed Newland and *Raising Faith Filled Kids: Ordinary Opportunities to Nurture Spirituality at Home* by Tom McGrath

Stories, Saints, and Scripture

R eview any published catechetical curriculum and supplementary resource materials, and you will see that stories from everyday life, incidents from the lives of the saints, and passages from Scripture are integrated throughout the program.

Both the General and National Directories for Catechesis give extensive coverage to the importance of a diversity of methods, human experience, memorization, and the role of the catechist. Authors Carl J. Pfeifer and Janaan Manternach emphasize that story is one of the most powerful resources available for teaching religion. Stories have been used throughout history to teach, inspire, guide, and help people better understand themselves and their mission in life. The Old Testament is filled with stories used to convey God's love and faithfulness to Israel. In the Gospels, Jesus used parables to teach. The prominent author and storyteller, Madeline L'Engle wrote, "Jesus was not a theologian. He was God who told stories."

Over the last few years a great variety of biographies and books on saints for both adults and children have been published. The lives of the saints and other virtuous men and women provide inspiration, encouragement, and guidance in living the Gospel every day. It is for this reason that all catechetical programs include examples and biographies of saints.

Finally, one of the most important responsibilities of the catechist is to foster in children a knowledge and love of Sacred Scripture. In religion class, a catechist needs to use whatever means available to make God's Word come alive for the children, to demonstrate that Bible reading is part of every Christian's life, and to show that the Sacred Scripture is the source of prayer and devotions. It is also important to introduce and to celebrate the Lectionary as the way the Church parcels out Scripture to be read at the Sunday assembly and throughout the week.

We recommend that every child over the age of nine should have a Bible of his or her own. It should be treated as a prized possession. It is at this age that children are first open to reading the Bible and they will make it a part of their practice of the faith. It is ideal if the children receive the Bible as a gift from the parish—their family of faith.

> The Church, in transmitting the faith does not have a particular method nor any single method. Rather, she discerns contemporary methods in the light of the pedagogy of God and uses with liberty "everything that is true, ...everything that we love and honor and everything that can be thought virtuous or worthy of praise" *(Philippians 4:8).*
>
> *General Directory for Catechesis,* 148

How Creative Catechists Use Stories by Janaan Manternach and Carl J. Pfeifer and *The Loyola Kids Book of Saints* by Amy Welborn

Quick Hits

Children's Literature

Most catechists' editions include recommendations for children's literature that connect thematically to a particular lesson. We encourage you to use these. Children love stories, particularly read-to-me stories. Often a story is the best way to make connection to more abstract teaching. Spend an afternoon in the children's section of your local library—just browsing through books. You are sure to find some that you can use throughout the year.

Nurturing a Spiritual Awareness

It is a far greater challenge for adults than it is for children to be spiritually aware. Children have an almost intuitive awareness of the spiritual. Hone your own spiritual awareness by observing them. How is God present to you through them? Then, you will be able to help the children continue to experience God's presence in them and in the world around them.

The Catechist-Home Connection

The Church expects a lot of parents. They hear over and over again that they bear the prime responsibility for the religious formation of their young ones, and then they get precious little help. That leads us to the current hot topic in catechetical circles—*adult* faith formation. As one catechetical leader put it, "Parents have been neglected for so long! It is hard to *stop* neglecting them."

One thing we have found ourselves pretty good at over the years— blaming parents. We blame them when the children are absent, and we blame them when children are late. We blame them if they don't participate in parent meetings (especially for sacramental preparation), and we blame them if they hang around too much.

Parents really do care about the faith formation of their children. However, they live in a very hectic world. So, how do parents fit into your life as a catechist? How do you help them fulfill their "prime directive" without laying just another unsupported burden on their shoulders?

We are not suggesting that you become the champion family minister of the world, but we are suggesting that there are simple things you can do to be aware of the needs of parents in your program. Read on for a few.

Parent Meetings

Many parents dread parent meetings with the catechist or the DRE. As one parent summed it up (a little too frankly), "Either they lecture us for an hour and a half on the history of the sacraments, or put they us in small groups and tell us to talk to one another about stuff I'm not all that comfortable sharing with strangers. Frankly, I don't know which is worse. At least during the lecture I can nod off. I can't skip the meeting because if I don't go, my daughter won't be able to receive her First Communion."

Parent meetings are important. They can be effective, too, if you plan them around the needs of the parents and not around your needs or the needs of the program. You may be excited about a tour-de-force history of the Sacrament of Reconciliation. In all likelihood the history is not on the parent's need-to-know list. At the same time, a parent may want to know about forgiveness in the family, getting in the habit of frequent confession, ways to talk about things that go wrong at home, and the like.

If you want a good parent meeting, ask the parents what they want and need to hear—before the meeting, not after it. In short, treat the parents like adults. And in the meetings:

- Use a variety of learning approaches. Adults learn in a variety of ways.
- Include opportunities for group participation, but never force participation.
- Use the expertise of your participants. Your parents will love you for this. Tap the rich resource that they can be for one another—and for you—as they share insights about their faith, their parenting roles, and their children.

To be a person of living faith is an ongoing challenge. Engage your participants in real-life problem solving where faith influences life! Never, ever tell parents that their child will be denied a sacrament if they (the parents) do not show up at a meeting. This is just plain wrong. You cannot deny a child his or her right to a sacrament because a parent misses a meeting.

Be considerate of the life situations of your parents, recognize their needs, and watch them show up!

> By means of personal contact, meetings, courses, and also adult catechesis directed toward parents, the Christian community must help them assume their responsibility—which is particularly delicate today—of educating their children in the faith.
> *General Directory for Catechesis 227*

 Youth Worker's Guide to Parent Ministry by Marv Penner

Meeting Parents

Our experience has taught us that every catechetical series includes parent materials. That same experience tells us that they are very often an afterthought. Every subject in the curriculum now has a school-to-home strategy. That means that on any give day, parents with two children in school get four to ten activity sheets that are supposed to make them more a part of the children's education. Then the kids come home from catechism and (Look!) another activity sheet.

So I encourage you, your fellow catechists, and the faith formation director to ask the parents what they need from the program. By your willingness to listen and to adapt, you will help parents realize that they share faith by being parents, not by running extra catechism classes in the evening at home. You assure them that you are doing the best job possible to do the formal catechesis. Then follow some of the hints below.

1. At the beginning of the catechetical year, share with both the parents and the entire parish what the children will be learning at each level. Keep it simple—just a few sentences. Include the notice in the Sunday bulletin, the parish website, and notes *mailed* to the home.
2. Offer tips for sharing faith at home by suggesting specific Bible stories, children's literature, lives of the saints, and prayers for family and children to share at dinner, in the evening, or in the morning.
3. Other helps might be letters or e-mails with quick suggestions for family conversation or simple questions that will help the family discover the readings for the coming Sunday.

4. Join together with other catechists and the director to develop a one page quarterly e-newsletter. Offer practical and realistic suggestions for sharing faith. Use the various resources that are available from a variety of publishers. Keep it simple and practical.

In short, here is what Catholic parenting for faith entails:
* *Tell and retell the biblical story—the stories of faith-together.*
* *Celebrate faith and life every day.*
* *Pray together.*
* *Listen, talk, and forgive one another.*
* *Perform acts of faithful service and witness together.*

> But speaking the truth in love, we must grow up in every way into him who is the head, into Christ, from whom the whole body joined and knit together by every ligament with which it is equipped, as each part is working properly, promotes the body's growth in building itself up in love.
>
> *Ephesians 4:15-16*

☑ *Bringing Up Children in the Christian Faith* by John H. Westerhoff, III (E-book format, available from www.faithAlivebooks.com)

Not the Enemy

Sometimes it is a temptation to make parents the enemy. Catechists seem to be competing with every other thing a family has to do—school activities, sports, family activities, or extra-curricular work. And sometimes we all feel that the religion class is losing the competition. And of course, that must be the parents' fault.

Every catechist needs to fight the feeling that parents are the enemy. I received a phone call one morning from the DCM (Director of Catechetical Ministry) at the parish. She said hello and then proceeded to tell me how negligent my husband and I were for not showing up at the mandatory meeting for First Communion parents the night before. She even hinted that our daughter might not be able to receive her First Communion. I listened, and when she was through, this is what I told her. "Yesterday we were at the funeral of my dad—our daughter's grandfather. After his funeral we went to the hospital to visit my mother-in-law, who is in intensive care. Somehow, I think these were more important things for my husband and me to be doing than attending your meeting at the parish." Clearly, this leader's focus was on the importance of her meeting, and not on the lives of the families the meeting was intended to embrace. Yes, she was apologetic. My hope is that she did adjust her attitude, and began seeing parents as partners in faith formation, not competitors. Perhaps she has since adopted a more sensitive family perspective.

The children you work with and their families have many things vying for their attention. Look for simple ways to connect with the home, and show that you care. Be an advocate for families.

If all the members of the Church are to follow Christ's way of love, it is essential that we continue speaking with, listening to, and learning from each other. We are the one Body of Christ: the Church in the home, in the small community, in the parish, in the diocese, in a universal communion. We share one Lord, one faith, one baptism. We are one family in Christ!

Follow the Way of Love

Follow the Way of Love: A Pastoral Message to Families by the United States Conference of Catholic Bishops

Faith at Home

The *National Directory for Catechesis* gives parents a most important catechetical role—to be good Catholic parents. The directory points out that parents catechize primarily by the witness of their Christian lives and their own love of the Faith. The love and respect that parents have for each other is another catechetical lesson. Faith at home—the "domestic church"—revolves around the ordinary stuff of life. It is not so much tested and measured by quizzes and discussion groups as it is by the teachable moments of tears and triumphs, of prayers and parties, of shared meals and remembered anniversaries. The vigil at the bed of a sick child is a catechetical lesson, as is the family Bible enshrined in a special corner. The weekly trip to the parish church for Sunday Mass is as much a lesson as is the homily or the discussion group after Mass. Faith at home is the hot thermos of soup taken to the gentleman around the corner who can't get out much any more.

So what's a catechist to do? Recognize that not you or anybody puts Christ into the Christian home. He is there all the time. Little things you do serve to pull back the veil and increase awareness. Here are three little tips.

Send Stuff Home: Not just more work, mind you. Send home the artwork the children have done. Send a meal prayer that the children wrote and laminated for use at the table. How about a prayer candle decorated by the child?

Be a Resource. Your director of faith formation can be a big help with this. Parishes can be great clearinghouses for all sorts of resources that benefit families—from books and videos in the parish libraries to a listing of various organizations in your community that promote Catholic family living.

And Again—Meet Them: Make sure they are real people to you—moms and dads, brothers and sisters. Greet them by name when you see them in the parish and community.

Be the face of your parish to these families of faith.

> Parish life itself is an aid to parents because it is here, at the Eucharistic banquet, that Christ himself nourishes them. The vibrancy of the parish community, the beauty of worship, and the example of generous love and service of parishioners strengthens parents in the faith.
>
> *National Directory for Catechesis, page 235*

 Family Faith Communities by Amy Sluss

Interfaith Families

A few decades ago, in the days of Catholic neighborhoods, catechists could assume that both parents in the families of the children in their programs were Catholic. Today almost half of Catholic marriages are interfaith marriages. The children you teach may experience more than one religious tradition at home. Or they may have one or both parents not participating at the parish. They may have a parent who is interested in the Catholic Church and considering becoming a Catholic.

"What," you may ask, "does this have to do with me as a catechist?" Even in a marriage in which both mom and dad are Catholic, religious education is not easy. But in an interfaith marriage the religious education of the child can become a source of conflict. Here are a few things you may be able to do to support these families.

1. Recognize that the more the parents learn about each other's faiths, the stronger the faith foundation will be at home. Invite these parents to attend various adult faith formation events your parish offers. The faith formation approach a parish adopts can influence how comfortable the non-Catholic parent feels in learning about the Catholic faith.
2. Recognize that interfaith families will find worship patterns that fit the faiths and the family. In fact, it is important for them to find the appropriate pattern of how they will worship. This can be a struggle, so be sure not to add to the tension by voicing your own judgments on the ways the families work this out.

3. Encourage your parish to consider a process for reflection and decision-making about these issues in the baptismal preparation program.
4. Encourage interfaith parents to take the religious education of their children seriously. After all, passing on a strong tradition and values and belief system is something interfaith parents would want to do.
5. Provide simple prayers that the family can pray at home. Common prayer can unite the interfaith family.

The interfaith families of your students provide a great opportunity to model ecumenical understanding and discovery.

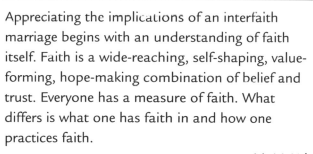

Appreciating the implications of an interfaith marriage begins with an understanding of faith itself. Faith is a wide-reaching, self-shaping, value-forming, hope-making combination of belief and trust. Everyone has a measure of faith. What differs is what one has faith in and how one practices faith.

Iris M. Yob

 Keys to Interfaith Parenting by Iris M. Yob, Ed.D.

Family Strengths

The home of every one of your students, regardless of its structure, economic level, ethnic background, or cultural background, is a learning environment and (from a catechetical perspective) a school of faith. To build an effective partnership between your faith formation efforts and that of the home, you can tap into family strengths.

Who has a more intimate knowledge of the students you teach than their parents do? No one. Parents know more about their children's needs, skills, and interests than anybody else does. The insights they have to offer can enrich your efforts. Catechists seldom ask parents about their children—what they love to do, what they get excited about, what their special interests are. As a result, children in religion class often feel disconnected.

A family lives all the themes of faith day after day, year after year, in both the ordinary and extraordinary events of family life. The family experience is fertile ground for faith connections.

Children have an easy spirituality, and often they teach their parents about God—sometimes without their parents actually realizing it. Parents often learn about God by watching their children grow.

Parents want what is best for their children, and this includes what is best in spiritual matters. Have you ever heard a parent say that he or she wants to raise an evil child? Parishes can safely assume that parents want their children to grow up to be happy, healthy, and holy adults. Most parents want to work with the parish for their child's benefit. However, they don't want to play tug-of-war with you, which can happen if parishes fail to recognize family strengths.

Parents are the first source of faith formation. From the first time parents trace a sign of the cross on a child's forehead till the moment they close their eyes in eternal rest in the embrace of their children, parents hand on a love for Christ and a love for his Church.

> Family life is full of major and minor crises—the ups and downs of health, success and failure in career, marriage, and divorce—and all kinds of characters. It is tied to places and events and histories. With all of these felt details, life etches itself into memory and personality. It's difficult to imagine anything more nourishing to the soul.
>
> *Thomas Moore*

 Experiencing God with Your Children by Kathy Coffey

What Do Parents Want?

T he majority of parents find life filled to the brim with earning a living, taking care of family responsibilities, mundane tasks and chores, and (if they are lucky) even a little rest and relaxation. In addition to that full and active life, Catholic parents want to make sure that their home is a place of faith. They often take the time (or would with a little help) to share faith as a family—offering a mealtime blessing, praying with their children at bedtime, faithfully attending Mass, and making sure that the children get religious instruction.

The *National Directory for Catechesis* stresses how important it is that while young children receive their initial catechesis in the home by sharing Christian values, praying with their children, and reading and sharing stories from Scripture. The Directory also states that school-aged children should receive a formal and systematic catechesis that presents the principal mysteries of the Catholic faith, the teachings and ministry of Jesus Christ, and a sacramental catechesis for Penance and the Eucharist.

Here are a few answers to the question "What do you want from your parish?"
- Recognize that children are the Church. Listen to them. Help channel their energy into participation in the parish.
- Create a parish that is centered on the Eucharist with strong adult formation and with enlightened and intelligent homilies.
- Build a community in which children can experience a Christ-centered world.

- Offer a welcoming and engaging program for teens.
- Provide participation in the liturgy and in programs promoting justice and peace.
- Help make a parish that is part of our lives, not just a place we go to on Sunday morning.
- Make available resources for family prayer and intergenerational events.

Working together we can create a church that provides for the nourishment of both parents and children and a place where young people can "hang" with their peers.

Across the nation is a growing movement to strengthen and support family life. Men and women are sharing the responsibilities of parenting, and fathers' and mothers' roles have become more flexible.

National Directory for Catechesis, page 36

 Generations of Faith Project by the Center for Ministry Development

Practicing Catholic

Who is a practicing Catholic, anyway? The first response is "a person who regularly attends Mass on Sunday and contributes to the support of the Church."

Regular participation in Sunday liturgy is one of the many practices that are important in the life of Catholics. But the definition of *practicing* needs also to include a more comprehensive list of beliefs, attitudes, behaviors, and practices.

The catechetical writer Thomas Groome gives a list of attitudes and sensibilities that show a practicing Catholic:
• A positive understanding of the human person
• Commitment to community
• A sacramental outlook
• Love and appreciation of both Scripture and tradition
• A faith that involves head, heart, and hands
• Commitment to justice
• A "universal" spirituality—open and outgoing
• A welcoming and inclusive approach to the Church
• Devotion to Mary

In our relationship with parents, we need to witness to these characteristics and be a catalyst to help families "practice" their faith.

There is a pun hidden in the words "practicing faith."
It can mean that we keep doing things over and over
until we get it all right!

As the believer progresses on the journey toward the Father in the footsteps of Christ under the guidance of the Holy Spirit, catechesis should deepen the believer's understanding of the mystery of Christ.

National Directory for Catechesis, page 95

 What Makes Us Catholic: Eight Gifts for Life by Thomas H. Groome

Quick Hits

In the Beginning—the Parents

And God saw that they were good! Parents are wonderful creations of God. They have a daunting job to do (without God's grace—near impossible.) They need love and support and encouragement, and even though they might forget to tell you, they are appreciative of what you offer their children. All faith-filled parents want their children to know and be loved by other adults who know, love, and serve God. So partner with the parents of the children you teach, as you all grow in faith together.

The Families Not in Church

You are not in *control* of parents. The alarming statistic that almost two out of three Catholics do not attend Mass weekly can add a "What's the use?" to your list of catechetical woes. What you can do is provide a positive example to the children you teach, and turn the rest over to God. Perhaps by your caring witness, some families will start showing up at the 10:30 Mass on Sunday. You don't get that response from a harsh note sent home with the kids. You might with a good welcoming attitude and an occasional "Come and see!"

The Catechist-Parish Connection

When you are in the classroom with the children, it may seem at times like you stand there all alone. Of course you're not. But that doesn't help when all you really want to do is poke your head out the door and scream at the top of your lungs, "Help!"

As a catechist, you're never alone. You are a part of a faith community that, we hope, takes very seriously its role as transmitter of faith. This means the children you teach are a part of a bigger community, too—the community of the parish. You share with your class the bigger picture about what the Church believes and teaches and how the parish lives all that out as a faith community—alive and well in the world.

Good things are happening out there. We want to remind you of a few of them.

A Parish on Life Support!

While we'd love to believe that all of the more than 19,000 Catholic parishes in the United States are vibrant, life-giving, nurturing centers of personal and communal spiritual growth, we know it just isn't so. If you muttered under your breadth, "That's *my* parish...." when you read the title on this page, then you know the catechetical struggle we're addressing: "I can be as creative and effective in the classroom setting as possible, but if the children don't experience the adventure of faith in the broader parish community, what's the use?"

Instead of dwelling on the fact that your parish may be less than lively, consider what you, as a catechist in your parish, might be able to influence. For example, what if you and the children in your program or class took snapshots of each other, created a bright poster of all your smiling faces, and put it in a gathering place at the church? Better yet, how about showcasing via photos the families of all the children in your class? Other parishioners, seeing such a display, would subconsciously think, "There are things going on around here." What if every week you asked your class for their top ten list of things to pray for, and then offered these petitions to the person responsible for putting together the Prayers of the Faithful for the coming Sunday? You can subtly suggest that one or two of these prayers be included at liturgy on the coming Sunday.

Catechists can have a great influence in the life of the parish. They can help to demonstrate that the Spirit is alive and well in the parish. Meet with some of your catechist friends and brainstorm ideas that might work. As the saying goes, "Throw them against the wall and see if they stick." Some won't, but others will.

Don't underestimate your own ability to show that the Spirit is alive in your parish!

> The process of continuing conversion goes beyond what is provided by basic catechesis. In order to encourage this process, it is necessary to have a Christian community which welcomes the initiated, sustains them and forms them in the faith: Catechesis runs the risk of becoming barren if no community of faith and Christian life welcomes the catechumen at a certain stage of his catechesis.
>
> *General Directory for Catechesis 69*

☑ *Called to Be Stewards: Bringing New Life to Catholic Parishes* by Patrick H. McNamara

A Just Parish

Years ago, in my early days in ministry, I was at a workshop on the Church and social justice. I wrote this note on the program, "There are more books on the social teaching of the Church than in any other subject area in Catholicism." I never tried to verify the statement, but the impact has stayed with me for years. Our Church has a whole lot to say about social justice. This was evident in a big way in the news coverage after the death of Pope John Paul II—a champion of basic human rights and dignity.

Each parish is responsible for sharing that social teaching with its members and for living out the Church's responsibility to foster justice and peace.

The United States bishops point out seven key social-justice themes:

- *The Life and Dignity of the Human Person:* This belief is so central to the Church that much of her social teaching springs from it. The sanctity of each person and his or her creation in God's image is the foundation of a moral vision of society.
- *The Call to Family, Community, and Participation:* We have a social nature. We live in community and realize our dignity and sacredness in relationships.
- *The Rights and Responsibilities of the Human Person:* Every person has a right to life and a right to human decency—the right to food, shelter, clothing, employment, health care, and education. It is society's responsibility to protect and provide for those needs.
- *An Option for the Poor and Vulnerable:* How a society treats its most vulnerable members is a barometer of that society's morality.

- *The Dignity of Work and Rights of Workers:* God has given each person unique gifts for the service of others. Workers have a right to dignity and a just wage. Economies exist to serve the people, not the other way around.
- *The Solidarity of the Human Family:* All people, regardless of race, ethnicity, culture, or religion, have a common origin and a common destiny.
- *Care for God's Creation:* God has entrusted the world to people to be its stewards. We are creation's caretakers.

> The Church's social teaching is a rich treasure of wisdom about building a just society and living lives of holiness amidst the challenges of modern society.
>
> *United States Conference of Catholic Bishops*

✔️ *Catholic Social Teaching: Our Best Kept Secret* by Edward P. DeBerri and others

Parish-Wide Catechesis

Whole-community catechesis is one of the latest catch phrases in religious education circles. One can't go to a workshop or institute or diocesan conference without hearing about it. A catechist just has to ask, "So what is it, and what's it got to do with me?"

Whole-community catechesis, or parish-wide catechesis, is an approach to parish faith formation that is grounded in the documents of Vatican II, the Rite of Christian Initiation of Adults, and the *General Directory for Catechesis*. It is an approach that invites parishioners of all ages into the process of faith formation. The focus is on the whole parish, not just the kids. And, of course, involvement of the adults is integral.

This approach tightly integrates the Sunday liturgy to catechesis, both in the classroom and in the parish itself. The Liturgy of the Word is the starting point from which catechesis, reflection, and sharing about faith flows. Typically, faith-sharing groups of all ages discuss the word based on a "Question of the Week" which springs from the Sunday Scripture readings.

The transformational power of this paradigm of faith formation is already being experienced in many parishes. No longer are the catechist and student the only touch points for faith formation. Parish-wide catechesis opens up faith formation to the entire community and touches homes and families.

*With this vision of catechesis taking root across the country,
it is an exciting time to be a catechist!*

The Christian community is the origin, locus, and
goal of catechesis. Proclamation of the Gospel
always begins with the Christian community and
invites man to conversion and the following of
Christ.

General Directory for Catechesis, 254

Whole Community Catechesis in Plain English by Bill Huebsch and
The Gospel for All Ages by Joan Mitchell, CSJ

What Is Generations of Faith?

*O*ver one thousand parishes across the country are implementing an approach entitled Generations of Faith, so chances are this approach has come or soon will be coming to a parish near you! There are also other approaches that are similar and they are all good, solid attempts to spread catechesis throughout the parish.

Generations of Faith is event-centered, life-long, intergenerational faith formation. It focuses on the parish as an intergenerational learning community centered on the events of church life. It rests on the assumption that the Church itself, namely the events of Church life—Church year, liturgy and prayer, sacraments, justice and service—provide the perfect curriculum for growing in faith. This approach immerses people into the life of the Church and the rhythm of the Church year.

This approach requires a shift from a schooling model to a whole-church approach, where catechesis happens in large parish-wide events that prepare the community to celebrate an event of the Church, such as a Holy Day, a feast day, a church season. Thousands of catechists across the country have made the transition from classrooms to these intergenerational catechetical sessions that are a key part of the Generations approach. Here are the principles that guide the Generations of Faith approach.

1. *Event-centered.* The catechetical experiences revolve around the events of the Church year, the Sacraments and liturgy, prayer and spirituality, justice and service, community life, and the proclamation of the Word.

2. *Lifelong and Cyclic*. The approach taps into the natural rhythm and pattern of the faith community's life throughout the year.
3. *Emergent*. The beliefs and practices of the Church are embedded in the life and events of the Church year. This principle recognizes that the curriculum or "content" emerges from the event.
4. *Alignment*. Because this life-long formation focuses the entire faith community on events of Church life and of the Church year, all ages are focused at the same time on the same theological theme.
5. *Home Faith Formation*. Supporting and nurturing faith growth in the households of the parish is the essence of the approach.

There are other strategies for intergenerational catechesis. One is *The Gospel for all Ages* from Pflaum Publishing Group. This strategy employs the weekly lectionary-based handouts from Pflaum and from Good Ground Press.

> Catechesis is nothing other than the process of transmitting the Gospel, as the Christian community has received it, understands it, celebrates it, lives it, and communicates it in many ways.
>
> *General Directory for Catechesis, 105*

☑ *The Pflaum Gospel Weeklies*—www.pflaum.com, *Sunday by Sunday* and *Spirit*—www.goodgroundpress.org, and Generations of Faith—www.generationsoffaith.org

Help Is on the Way

Parish catechists volunteer for a variety of reasons:
- "I want to learn more about my faith."
- "I have a child in the program and I would like to be a witness for her."
- "Our parish is so big, and this will give me the opportunity to meet a few new people."
- "I have something to offer, and I want to share that with others."

Once catechists are recruited and volunteer, however, the entire parish community is called to support and care for them, so that they can be successful and effective in this ministry.

Terri, a lifelong catechist and a parish director of adult faith formation, encourages catechists to be open and to rely on the Holy Spirit. "Just as catechists pray for guidance, strength, and insight, the parish community is called to continually pray for and support all their catechists."

Each year the church in the United States celebrates Catechetical Sunday on the third weekend in September. This day should be a parish festival of catechesis. It can be an opportunity to recognize and commission catechists, to bless parents and guardians in their roles, and remind every single member of the parish of the responsibility to support the catechetical ministry. But for catechists to minister well, they need support all year long—not just on Catechetical Sunday.

The *National Directory for Catechesis* outlines the responsibilities of the diocesan bishop, priests, pastors, and catechetical leaders. They are to foster a sense of common responsibility for catechesis in the Christian community—a task that involves all and includes a formal recognition and appreciation for catechists and their mission.

Bishop Howard J. Hubbard of Rochester reminds his catechists, "yours is a mission and ministry that is vitally essential to the church and one of enormous importance as you set the tone for how the Good News is proclaimed, reflected upon, discussed, and put into practice through prayer, worship, and service."

Catechists are encouraged to look to their pastor and catechetical leaders for curriculum guidance; for their formation and training; for adequate resources; and for opportunities to ask questions, to seek direction, and to gather together.

As the entire parish community offers prayer, support, and recognition, the pastor and catechetical leaders provide both individualized assistance and overall direction for all aspects of the catechetical ministry.

> Seek advice from every wise person and do not despise any useful counsel. At all times bless the Lord God, and ask him that your ways may be made straight and that all your paths and plans may prosper.
>
> *Tobit 4:18-19*

 I Am Bread Broken: A spirituality for the Catechist by Howard J. Hubbard

The Catechetical Leader

Not long after the Second Vatican Council, parishes across the country began hiring directors of religious education. These people worked in parishes developing and managing catechetical programs for adults, youth, children, and families. At the same time, there was a renewed commitment to the study and reading of Sacred Scripture, and to the updating of the celebration of the sacraments and liturgy. The documents of the Council spoke about the Church as a people of God, about a universal call to holiness, about the laity, and about the mission of the Church in the modern world.

In collaboration with the pastor and other parish ministers, there emerged a new ministry—the director of religious education. Today this director (known often as a DRE, a catechetical leader, a director of faith formation) is responsible for catechesis, sacramental preparation, and the RCIA for the parish. Most parishes have a catechetical leader.

In addition to the organizing and managing of the program one of the primary responsibilities of the director of religious education is to assist catechists in their preparation, training, education, and formation.

Here are a few things you can expect from your DRE or catechetical leader:

1. *Set Expectations:* What am I expected to teach? Be specific. What do we want the children know, appreciate, and do at the end of the year?

2. *Goals:* What are we striving for? How will we know we have accomplished what we set out to do?
3. *Structure:* What is the structure of our program? How do I fit in? How am I accountable?
4. *Mentoring:* Is there someone who can help me—show me what to do?
5. *Resources:* What books, articles, Web sites, or prayers and devotions do you recommend for my formation?
6. *In-Service Training:* How do I use the published program we have been given? Can you help me with Scripture?

Share your concerns and questions with the parish catechetical leader. He or she will be able to provide direction, information, and guidance to address your needs and help you become an effective catechist.

> The single most critical factor in an effective parish catechetical program is the leadership of a professionally trained parish catechetical leader.
>
> *National Directory for Catechesis, page 224*

 Effective DRE by Richard Reichert

No Catechist Left Behind

In the United States there are 500,000 volunteer catechists serving in almost 19,000 parishes. If the Catholic Church in the United States created a "No Catechist Left Behind" initiative, how might catechists be recruited, called, recognized, and supported for this sacred and critical parish ministry?

It is critical that parishes and dioceses throughout the country increase their commitment and resources to the implementation of extensive catechist formation. It is only then would no catechist be left behind.

In 2002 the United States Conference of Catholic Bishops issued a report entitled *Best Practices in Catechist Formation*. Data was collected from dioceses, parishes, and other institutions involved in catechist formation. Important principles emerged:

1. The most important ingredient for effective catechist formation is that bishops, pastors, and pastoral staffs recognize the importance of catechist formation and allocate resources.
2. An essential aspect for successful catechist formation is choosing the proper candidates. Recruitment is critical.
3. Formation needs to involve growing as a person of faith—knowing the message, knowing the audience, and knowing how to communicate the message effectively.
4. Dioceses and parishes need to work together to provide formation.
5. Successful catechist formation embraces diverse and flexible approaches.
6. Effective formation programs provide continuing encouragement for those in formation.

What is critical is that the members of each parish pastoral staff work together collaboratively, creatively, and continuously in the formation of catechists, helping people to develop a personal relationship with Jesus Christ.

Since effective catechesis depends on virtuous and skilled catechists, their ongoing formation should enhance the human, spiritual, and apostolic qualities and catechetical skills they bring to their ministry.
National Directory for Catechesis, page 238

Best Practices in Catechist Formation by the United States Conference of Catholic Bishops

National Directory for Catechesis

T hroughout this guide, you have seen mentioned over and over a
National Directory. Well what is it, anyway? The *National Directory
for Catechesis* is the most recent help for the catechetical ministry in
the United States. The United States Conference of Catholic Bishops
released it in May of 2005. The Directory will form, guide, and
encourage a renewal of catechetical ministry for years to come. These
two pages will give you a whirlwind tour of the Directory. Most of
this document is designed for leaders in catechesis. Nonetheless,
any catechist will harvest much good from its pages. If reading the
Directory does nothing else, it will give you a deep appreciation of
the challenge and the privilege of a call to catechetical ministry.

- *Introduction:* The introduction sets the vision for the Directory
  and for the renewal of catechesis.
- *Chapter 1—Proclaiming the Gospel in the United States:* This chapter
  covers the unique qualities of the United States—especially its
  diversity—and their influence on catechesis.
- *Chapter 2—Catechesis Within the Church's Mission of Evangelization:* This
  chapter gives the nature and purpose of catechesis, the tasks
  associated with it, and ways to inculturate the Gospel message.
- *Chapter 3—This is Our Faith; This Is the Faith of the Church:* This chapter
  outlines the content of the catechetical message.
- *Chapter 4—Divine and Human Methodology:* This chapter shows God's
  own pedagogy and discusses the many and varied methods at the
  catechist's disposal.

- *Chapter 5—Catechesis in a Worshiping Community:* This chapter covers the relationship between the liturgy and catechesis—especially Christian Initiation.
- *Chapter 6—Catechesis for Life in Christ:* This long chapter discusses moral formation and the formation of a Christian conscience.
- *Chapter 7—Catechizing the People of God in Diverse Settings:* This chapter discusses the catechetical mission at the different ages and stages of people's lives.
- *Chapter 8—Those Who Catechize:* This chapter shows the responsibility of the bishop and all who share the ministry with him. It also outlines catechist formation.
- *Chapter 9: Organizing Catechetical Ministry:* This chapter shows how best to structure this ministry for effectiveness and faithfulness.
- *Chapter 10—Resources for Catechesis:* This chapter covers all the various resources that are available as sources of formation and for instruction.
- *Conclusion:* The conclusion demonstrates a renewed passion for catechesis and calls on the Holy Spirit (the Teacher within) and the Virgin Mary (the Star of Evangelization) to support this ministry in the United States.

This Directory will be a valuable asset for you in your ministry.

Quick Hits

The Warm Body Experience

It is the day before religion classes start. The call comes. Once again, the parish is short on catechists. Can you do it? Pleeeeease? No matching of your gifts to the needs of the program, just (hear the begging tone) "Pleeeeeease! We're stuck!" So you say yes, and you feel like a warm body, showing up, going through the motions, and darn it, you don't really want to be there. But you are, so we thought you'd like to know that God has a special place in heaven reserved for catechists like you. We don't know what this corner of heaven is like, but we're sure it's worth it.

Vatican II. What's That?

Vatican II was a Church council held from 1962-1965. It was one of the great events in the history of the Church. If you are a younger catechist (say under forty-five) you are probably tired of the older catechists saying "Vatican II this, and Vatican II that." Make a point of discovering more about the Second Vatican Council and its great challenges and changes. And rejoice in the fact that you are serving as a catechist in the Church today and that you are welcomed into full participation in the life and ministry of the Church. Hooray!

Resources

This list of recommended books focuses on titles for the ongoing education and formation of catechists, aides, and volunteers in the parish catechetical programs. As in the rest of this guide, we are giving just the title and author. With those two bits of information, you can find the books online or in any library or bookstore.

All Saints: Daily Reflections on Saints, Prophets, and Witnesses for Our Time by Robert Ellsberg

Best Practices in Catechist Formation by the United States Conference of Catholic Bishops

Called to Be a Catechist: Your Practical Guide by Cullen Schippe

Catechism of the Catholic Church

The Catechist's Companion: Planting, Watering, Growing by Cullen Schippe

Catechist magazine from Peter Li Education Group

The Catholic Faith Handbook For Youth by Brian Singer-Towns

The Discipline Guide for Children's Ministry by Jody Capehart, Gordon West, Becki West

Documents of Vatican II edited by Austin Flannery, OP

Documents of Vatican II in Plain English by Bill Huebsch

Effective DRE by Richard Reichert

continued on next page

Encyclopedia of Catholicism by Richard P. McBrien

The General Directory for Catechesis in Plain English by Bill Huebsch

How Creative Catechists Use Stories by Janaan Manternach and
  Carl J. Pfeifer

How to Talk so Kids Will Listen and Listen So Kids Will Talk by
  Adele Faber and Elaine Mazlish

I Am Bread Broken: A Spirituality for the Catechist by Howard J. Hubbard

I Like Being in Parish Ministry by Alison Berger

Invitation to Catholicism: Beliefs, Teachings, Practices by Alice Camille

*Invitation to the New Testament: A Catholic Approach to the Christian
  Scriptures* by Alice Camille

Invitation to the Old Testament: A Catholic Approach to the Hebrew Scriptures
  By Alice Camille

The Joy of Being a Catechist: From Watering to Blossoming by
  Gloria Durka, Ph.D.

The National Directory for Catechesis by the United States
  Conference of Catholic Bishops

The New American Bible (Concise) Concordance edited by
    John R. Kohlenberger III

New American Bible: Personal Study Edition, Oxford University Press

A New Look at Grace: A Spirituality of Wholeness by Bill Huebsch

Paths to Prayer by Robert F. Morneau

A Prayer Book for Catechists by Gwen Costello

Pocket Bible Guide by Linda Grenz

The Seeker's Guide to Reading the Bible: A Catholic View by Steve Mueller

To Teach As Jesus Did by the United States Conference of
    Catholic Bishops

What Makes Us Catholic: Eight Gifts for Life by Thomas H. Groome

When You Are a Catechist by Judith Dunlap

*Why Do They Act That Way? A Survival Guide to the Adolescent Brain for You
    and Your Teen* by David Walsh, Ph.D.

*Yardsticks: Children in the Classroom Ages 4–14, A Resource for
    Parents and Teachers* by Chip Wood

Web Sites

The following Web sites will provide you with a wealth of information and help in your catechetical ministry. They will also link you to hundreds of other resources.

American Catholic www.americancatholic.org
Catholic News Service www.catholicnews.com
Center for Media Literacy www.medialit.org
Center for Ministry Development www.cmdnet.org
Faith Alive Books www.faithAlivebooks.com
Home Faith www.homefaith.com
Learning Disabilities www.ldonline.org
The Movie Mom www.moviemom.com
National Institute on Media and the Family www.mediafamily.org
New American Bible www.usccb.org/nab/bible
Office of Social Justice, Archdiocese of St. Paul and Minneapolis www.osjspm.org
Online *Catechism of the Catholic Church* www.scborromeo.org/ccc.htm
Pauline Center for Media Studies www.daughtersofstpaul.com/mediastudies
Pflaum Publishing Group www.pflaum.com
Preparing for Sunday www.preparingforsunday.com
Responsive Classroom www.responsiveclassroom.org
Sunday by Sunday www.goodgroundpress.com
United States Conference of Catholic Bishops www.usccb.org